A
Time
for
Healing

Marie D. Jones, Anne Broyles,
Rebecca Christian, June Eaton,
Susan Farr Fahncke, Carol Smith,
Natalie Walker Whitlock

 Publications International, Ltd.

Louis Weber, CEO
Publications International, Ltd.
7373 North Cicero Avenue
Lincolnwood, Illinois 60712

Manufactured in U.S.A.

8 7 6 5 4 3 2 1

ISBN: 0-7853-9845-7

Contents

Starting Anew

Hope, like dawn, touches the darkness with light, opening us to the new day coming.

The steadfast love of the Lord never ceases,
his mercies never come to an end;
they are new every morning;
great is your faithfulness.
"The Lord is my portion," says my soul,
"therefore I will hope in him."

Lamentations 3:22–24

MY NEW BEGINNING

Today is my new beginning,
The past is over and gone,
However I got to this point,
From here I can only move on.
Though the road ahead be rocky,
And the future I cannot see,
I'll walk with my head held high,
With angels on each side of me.
Today is my new beginning,
And as I depart, I will pray,
That God will bless my journey,
And guide me each step of the way.

*A journey of a thousand miles begins with a
single step.*

Chinese proverb

A WHISPER IN THE WIND

The wind was blowing, and it looked like rain. The weather mirrored what was in Kaitlyn's heart. *If only I hadn't lost the baby,* she thought for the hundredth time that day.

The phone rang. It was Kaitlyn's husband, Mark, calling from his new job. "Honey, a few people from work are going bowling tonight. I think we should go."

Kaitlyn thought about it but just didn't feel up for it. "You go, honey. I'm just going to curl up by the fire with a good book," she said. They said their good-byes and hung up.

Kaitlyn looked down at her flat stomach and felt the sting of tears.

"Dear God, I don't think I can get through this," she said out loud. "Please help me."

She sighed, wondering how she should spend her afternoon. She decided to bake a pie, hoping it would lift her spirits.

She grabbed a basket, put on her jacket, and opened the front door. It met resistance from the wind. Kaitlyn pushed the door harder and went outside. She ran toward the old apple tree in her front yard. She picked a dozen or so apples and went back to the house. When she tried the door, she realized it had locked. *Great, this is just what I need.* She looked up at the darkening sky. She had no choice but to go to the neighbor's house.

A teenager opened the door. "Yeah?"

"I'm Kaitlyn Furrow, from next door. I've managed to lock myself out. May I use your phone?" The girl pointed to the phone, then plopped in front of the TV. Kaitlyn called Mark, who wouldn't be able to come home until 6:00.

> *So I tell you, whatever you ask for in prayer, believe that you have received it, and it will be yours.*
>
> Mark 11:24

"This is very awkward. My husband won't be home for a few hours. Could I possibly stay here until then?" she asked the teenage girl.

"Yeah, sure, whatever," the girl said without looking up.

Kaitlyn had an idea. "I have all these apples. Do you suppose it would be all right if I baked you a pie?"

"Uh-huh," came the reply.

As she searched for the ingredients, she heard footsteps bounding down the stairs. "I know you—you're the lady from next door!" Kaitlyn saw a little girl, about seven years old, standing in front of her.

"Jordan, isn't it?" Kaitlyn remembered having been introduced when they first moved in.

"Yes, and you're Kaitlyn. Can I help?" she asked eagerly.

"Of course, and maybe your sister would like to help, too." Kaitlyn looked toward the couch.

"That's not my sister, that's the baby-sitter, Emily," Jordan said with a giggle.

Kaitlyn put the ingredients on the counter, while Jordan searched for the measuring cups and spoons. "Here they are. Can I do it?" Jordan asked.

"Yes. I'll get the apples ready." Watching Jordan made Kaitlyn smile. She took her work very seriously. They rolled out the dough, and much of the flour ended up on Jordan.

"This is fun!" Jordan exclaimed.

While the pie was baking, Kaitlyn and Jordan cleaned the kitchen. "There, finished," Kaitlyn said.

"Will you read to me?" Jordan asked.

They sat at the kitchen table, and Kaitlyn read to her new friend. The apples and cinnamon made the kitchen wonderfully fragrant.

The door opened, and a gust of wind blew into the house. "Mommy!" Jordan yelled and ran to the door. She said, "Kaitlyn's here!" Kaitlyn stood up and started to explain. Before she could, the words tumbled out of Jordan's mouth, "She was picking apples, and the door slammed shut, so she came here, and we made a pie!"

Jordan's mother, Pam, walked over with her hand out. Her eyes went from Kaitlyn's face to her belly and back again. She nodded slightly, then said, "Pleased to see you again." She shook Kaitlyn's hand. "I've been meaning to come over, but I've been so...."

Emily interrupted as she headed for the door. "Oh, I forgot to tell you, I can't make it tomorrow." The door closed behind her.

"Kaitlyn can watch me!" Jordan said, enthusiastically.

Before Pam could object, Kaitlyn said, "I'd love to."

Pam saw the hopeful look on her daughter's face. "I think that might work out. Let's try it and see, okay?" she said. Jordan flew into her mother's arms and then into Kaitlyn's.

"Thank you, thank you, thank you!" she said. The deal was sealed over a slice of pie. Kaitlyn looked at her watch, then out the window. "Mark's home. I can see his car. I'll see you both tomorrow. Thanks."

As Kaitlyn walked across the yard to her house, she realized the wind had stopped. There was a small clearing in the clouds, and the sun peeked out a little. She looked up and thought, *Thank you, Lord. That was just what I needed.*

Mark opened the door. Kaitlyn smiled. "Do you think it's too late to go bowling?"

"No, that would be great. I know you'll like my new friends," Mark said.

God, I know you close some doors in my life in order to open new ones. I know things change and come to an end in order to leave room for new beginnings. Help me to have the boldness and enthusiasm to let go of the old and accept the new. Amen.

Hope assures us that what once was can be again.

At that time I will bring you home, at the time when I gather you; for I will make you renowned and praised among all the peoples of the earth, when I restore your fortunes before your eyes, says the Lord.

Zephaniah 3:20

Dear Father, we wonder why the pleasures of the past have left us. It is difficult to realize that they will be replaced by other pleasures. Please help us to trust in you as you reconstruct our lives. Amen.

The mind is like a garden of fertile soil into which the seeds of our thoughts, ideas, and intentions are planted. With loving care and nurturing attention, those seeds bloom forth to manifest in our lives as wonderful opportunities and events. Those seeds that we choose to either ignore or neglect will simply die off. Thus, our mind constantly turns over old growth into new. It is where we focus our energy and give our love that breaks through the dark soil into the light of day. It then becomes the visible good in our life, casting off new seeds to one day bloom forth in a cycle of renewal and abundance.

For there is hope for a tree, if it is cut down, that it will sprout again, and that its shoots will not cease.

Job 14:7

So if anyone is in Christ, there is a new creation: everything old has passed away; see, everything has become new!

2 Corinthians 5:17

Lord, your word created all there is. Let it now create a powerful restoration within me. Your love sustains all life. Let it now sustain and renew me. Your strength holds up the galaxies. Let it now hold me up and give me support. Your light reaches the far ends of the universe. Let it shine its healing energy upon me now. Amen.

JUST TEN DAYS

Never before had such a short amount of time seemed like an eternity to Ginger. She had only been sober for 20 days and now, as she looked forward to getting her monumental 30-day chip in Alcoholics Anonymous (AA), each moment was beginning to look insurmountable.

The cravings to take a drink were coming on stronger and stronger, and she found she needed to attend meetings twice a day—each morning and evening—just so she wouldn't give in to temptation. And then she had a lot of trouble sweating it out all night. In her former days, she would have been having a nightcap before bed. But now she read a little and then slept fitfully. She was trying to concentrate on other things—like sleeping—but her mind kept drifting and lingering on her desire for a drink.

She had fought this struggle one other time. After her mother had died, she had stopped drinking. But then she had begun to feel depressed and alone. And she felt guilty for not having spent more time with her mother. Then everything had seemed to be too much for Ginger, and she had started drinking again only two weeks later. She was happy that she had already been sober longer than the time before, but it was still hard to continue.

Ginger was trying to be determined, because this time she really had to quit. This time it was more than a milestone; it was a life-or-death decision. She was suffering from debilitating health problems that were directly related to her drinking. She could not have saved her and her mom's relationship, but she could save herself. She had to make it to her 30-day meeting, or she might end up in the hospital. She could even die.

> *From each of life's misfortunes, large or small, comes a new beginning, an opportunity to renew your faith in the future.*

Ginger had decided to join AA, and she lucked out on a great sponsor, Shirley. Shirley was a strong, assuring, religious woman. She was a real comfort to Ginger and helped Ginger place her trust in God. Ginger was beginning to feel better about herself and the world she lived in. With only ten days to go, Ginger prayed often and leaned hard on Shirley, who responded with kindness and firmness.

Nine days passed, and the very next day Ginger would receive her 30-day chip and be given a cake by her sponsor. Her new AA friends would be at the meeting as well as her family and some other friends. There were only 12 hours standing between Ginger and a new life of hope, healing, and courage.

But there was also the craving. She had had a terrible day at work and thought that a drink would help calm her nerves. She was coming very close to giving in. The desire to take just one sip was unbelievable. Although she had no liquor in her condo, she knew where all the local bars and convenience stores were. It would be so easy. No one would ever know.

No one but her, of course, and God. Instead Ginger did what Shirley had told her. She got out her AA phone list and called people and talked. The first few conversations began with her explaining her terrible day. After each one, she said a little prayer to God for help. She continued calling more and more people, and soon she was laughing and in a good mood. She had forgotten her terrible day. She then realized the craving had passed completely.

The very next morning, Ginger woke up and felt a rush of joy wash over her. She had made it to 30 days! And she realized that if she could make it through one month without drinking alcohol, she could make it through another.

She was so happy to have trusted God, especially because she had trouble trusting herself to not give in. She was also thankful for all of her supportive friends and family. She knew her days of loneliness were almost over, and she also knew she had a real chance to be whole again.

Ginger began to get dressed to go to the AA meeting. Every time she caught a glance of her face in the mirror, she noticed she was smiling uncontrollably. She couldn't help it, though, because she was so excited that she would soon receive her chip and cake proudly.

Lord, this healing process is sometimes slow, and I get discouraged and filled with doubt. Can I take this? Will I make it? Yet you always remind me of your powerful presence and assure me that where I am unable to go, you will go for me and what I am unable to do by myself, you will do for me. Thank you, Lord. Amen.

Change is never easy, but the blessings it bestows upon us are magnificent. Just ask the caterpillar struggling within the tight confines of a cocoon. Even as it struggles, it is becoming something glorious, something beautiful, soon to emerge as a winged butterfly. Change may bring temporary pain and discomfort, but it also brings the promise of a new life filled with joy and freedom and the ability to soar even higher than we ever did before.

God, we will try to learn and grow from challenges. We pray your promise of a new life can heal our wounds. We will try to remain patient because we know that you will cure us in good time. Amen.

Birds begin singing again before the storm has fully ended, having known all along that clouds cover—not banish—the sun.

SUN AND RAIN

Like sun that melts the snow,
my soul absorbs the grace
that beats in gentle, healing rays
from some godly place.
Like rain that heals parched earth,
my body drinks the love
that falls in gentle, soothing waves
from heaven up above.

A new beginning, like the breath of a heavenly being, makes the air a little sweeter and the world seem full of hope.

CLOSING THE DOOR

The entire family was exhausted. The fire had taken a toll on their spirits as well as their once beautiful home. Now their dream home stood with only two walls remaining, and their belongings were nothing but a rubble of ash and smoking embers.

For Lisa, the loss was especially devastating. This was the home she and her husband, Rick, had designed from scratch. This was the home where they had hoped to raise their two little girls. It had embodied all of their most special wishes for what a home truly could be, and little had been spared because of cost. Lisa and Rick felt that it would be their home forever, and they spent their entire savings on it.

But now Lisa stood facing what was left of her dreams, and the ache in her heart was immense. It was truly as if someone she loved and cherished had died.

The only thing left untouched by the raging fire was the front door, a massive oak double-door rimmed in a solid metal frame. It was, in fact, unscathed, and this sent a chill up Lisa's spine. How could the flames have not touched it? It was a question that would haunt her for a long time.

For the next two days, Lisa and Rick spent whatever time they could going through the rubble searching for anything that might have survived the fire. The days beyond that were spent flipping through insurance papers, but Lisa knew that no amount of money would rebuild the memories that house had afforded them. Rick tried to comfort Lisa, telling her that time would heal their pain and that they could—and would—rebuild a new home and new dreams.

Create in me a clean heart, O God, and put a new and right spirit within me.

Psalm 51:10

But Lisa could not let that house—and all it meant—go. Her heart became heavier, and she plunged into a deep depression, ignoring her health and appearance and spending less and less time with her daughters and Rick.

As the despair threatened to blacken her world forever, Lisa realized she would never heal from her loss until she could let it go. And she understood that letting go meant more than just coming to accept the loss in her mind. She had to let go physically. She had to do something, some act or ritual that would set the process of healing in motion.

It was their five-year-old daughter, Susan, who came up with the perfect idea. She had been listening to Lisa and Rick talk about their loss. Rick had been trying to console Lisa with the concept that when one door closes, another opens, when little Susan stepped forward and said in her high, meek voice, "Then we should go close the door."

It was such a simple yet profound statement, and it sent Lisa's heart soaring. She knew in that moment what she needed. They got into their car and went to the house, where the rubble had been surrounded with yellow *CAUTION* tape. The door was still standing there, looking quite out of place amidst the destruction.

Lisa walked her family to the door and opened it. They held hands, and each said a silent good-bye to their home and their memories of their lives there. Then Lisa stepped forward and closed the door.

It was one simple gesture, and to anyone looking at the family it probably seemed quite bizarre. But to Lisa, it was the beginning of healing and a whole new life.

Lord, I know that part of life is loss and that without loss we cannot treasure the new blessings that come our way. But I am still hurting, and the pain is deep. Help me to see the beautiful silver lining that surrounds the dark clouds now hanging overhead. Amen.

To let go is to live. Letting go opens the way for you to begin receiving more. Imagine a tree that refused to shed its dead leaves. Where would the new leaves find room to bloom forth in abundance? Without an outlet for new growth, eventually the whole tree suffers. By getting rid of the old to make way for the new, the whole tree benefits.

Blessed are those who trust in the Lord, whose trust is the Lord. They shall be like a tree planted by water, sending out its roots by the stream. It shall not fear when the heat comes, and its leaves shall stay green; in the year of drought it is not anxious, and it does not cease to bear fruit.

Jeremiah 17:7–8

The real voyage of discovery lies not in seeking new landscapes but in having new eyes.

Marcel Proust

God Almighty, please help me to put everything into perspective. I want to be realistic but also optimistic. Please send me hope and give me strength of mind to make things right again. Amen.

Hope has as many lives as a cat or a king.

Henry Wadsworth Longfellow

Accepting Truths

*Then you will know the truth, and
the truth will set you free.*

John 8:32 NIV

*Dear God, some of the greatest lessons we
learn are only after our hearts have suffered.
For in times of pain we receive wisdom, and
in times of sorrow we gain understanding.
This is your way of teaching our hearts that
we must know darkness in order to embrace
your light. Thank you for being our compassionate teacher. Amen.*

LIFT UP THINE EYES

Lift up thine eyes
to see the light
that heals the sick
and makes wrongs right.
Lift up thine heart
to feel the love
that emanates
from God above.

Faith flows as I stop depending on what I think, on what I feel, on what I see and instead embrace these facts: God loves me. He will never leave me. He wants only the best for me.

O most merciful Lord, grant to me thy grace, that it may be with me, and labour with me, and persevere with me even to the end. Grant that I may always desire and will that which is to thee most acceptable, and most dear. Let thy will be mine, and my will ever follow thine, and agree perfectly with it. Grant to me above all things that can be desired, to rest in thee, and in thee to have my heart at peace.

Thomas à Kempis

Encircle me in the arms of your love.
Fill me with your perfect peace.
Though my soul faints,
Sustain me through hope in your word.

JOURNEYS

When Harry came home from the hospital after his lung cancer surgery, an oxygen tank came with him. Even with the extra help, breathing and speaking were sometimes difficult. Walking was twice as hard. Yet Harry's doctor had told him that after the worst of the discomfort from the incision had subsided and he began healing,

Hard are the ways of truth, and rough to walk.

John Milton,
Paradise Regained

it would be important for Harry to stay as active as he could. "Use it or lose it," the doctor warned.

Harry loved nothing better than traveling with his wife of 50-some years, Lorna. So he was highly motivated to get well. Before he was able to get up and around, Lorna would sit beside him on the couch poring over brightly covered travel brochures. They discussed endless options for where they might go when the weather was warmer, when Harry was on the mend, and when he wouldn't need to use the oxygen tank as often.

Back to some of their old haunts, they mused, or maybe somewhere entirely new. Maybe they would even finally get to go on that trip to Europe while the fares were still low. As soon as Harry had a little breath and energy to spare, he began to walk around the house several times a day as the doctor had instructed, rolling his oxygen tank along. Lorna went with him, helping him adjust the tubing and watching out for the cord.

So boring was this routine that Harry was apologetic to Lorna. "You don't have to do this with me," he urged. "Get out to lunch with the girls. I'm fine." But Lorna wouldn't hear of it.

Then Harry came up with the idea of naming each room in the house after a favorite travel destination. The family room became North Carolina. When Harry got winded and had to rest on the couch for a few minutes, they pretended they were eating on the porch of their favorite country bed and breakfast, sipping a freshly squeezed lemonade and watching the sun set on the green hills. The guest room with its paintings of beaches and statues of lighthouses was Cape Cod. There they reminisced about their favorite place to get fried clams. Lorna sang bits of a song they both liked to Harry: "You're going to fall in love with old Cape Cod." The living room was New York because they could watch the neighborhood bustle from their picture window. There they remembered the first time, as twenty-somethings, they had visited Manhattan and gone to the top of the Empire State Building. A brisk wind had torn off Harry's hat and Lorna's chiffon scarf, and they had been too broke to replace them.

Lorna was overjoyed when Harry began to recover, traveling the circuit more times each day, needing the oxygen less. When Thanksgiving came they rejoiced at his progress and talked about visiting New England in the spring.

The day of the first snow came suddenly and without warning. It was on that day that Harry started the familiar circuit but paused, his breathing labored and his face ashen. He was hospitalized immediately with double pneumonia. A few days later, he died.

Lorna was heartbroken that Harry had started on his final journey without her. But as she began her own journey through the inhospitable landscape of grief, she was sustained not only by the memories of their most extravagant and exotic trips when Harry was well, but even more so by the laughter and love of the trips they had taken in those last weeks through the rooms of their own home.

God, please help me to accept your itinerary for my life's journey no matter where it brings me. I will wait for you to decide when I should return to your home. Amen.

Be brave, my soul—
Let go of lies.
Stop deceiving yourself.
Have courage
to embrace the truth
and all its consequences.

*Move our hearts with the calm, smooth flow
of your grace. Let the river of your love run
through our souls. May my soul be carried
by the current of your love, towards the
wide, infinite ocean of heaven. Stretch out
my heart with your strength, as you stretch
out the sky above the earth. Smooth out any
wrinkles of hatred or resentment. Enlarge
my soul that it may know more
fully your truth.*

Gilbert of Hoyland

The time of healing is a period of discovery about who we truly are, what we are made of, and what we can endure.

Lord, we understand that there are and will be problems in our lives, but please remind us of your presence when the problems seem insurmountable. We want to believe that you know best. We hope to remain patient as we search for purpose. Amen.

You have heard of the endurance of Job, and you have seen the purpose of the Lord, how the Lord is compassionate and merciful.

James 5:11

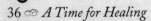

If we can face the past with acceptance, the present with confidence, and the future with expectancy, then we have the faith it takes for life's journey.

Heavenly Father, when I was young, I thought all things hurt or broken could be fixed: knees, feelings, bicycles, tea sets. Now I've learned that not everything can be repaired, relieved, or cured. As a mother comforts her child, heal my hurting and grant me the peace I used to know. This I pray. Amen.

Faith perceives a truth that lies beyond our field of vision—a truth only our heart has eyes to see.

FACE FORWARD

Rhoda could not believe she had skin cancer. She had always avoided the sun for fear of ruining her skin, but now she was faced with the prospect of having a large mole removed from her left cheek. The surgery would be quick, but it was the recovery that worried Rhoda. She would be permanently scarred in a place that would be difficult to hide, even with makeup.

The biopsy of her mole had come back malignant, and Rhoda understood it was imperative she have the surgery soon. It was scheduled for two days later, and she was a good little soldier, following all the doctor's directions and getting through the surgery with little complaint. But no one—not her doctor, mother, or sister, all of whom were present at the surgery— knew the pain she was suffering inside.

For a single young woman of 23, having a large facial scar was like death itself. Rhoda's self-esteem wasn't so hot to begin with, and now she was going to have a very difficult time facing anyone, especially on a date.

Three days after the surgery, Rhoda's doctor removed her bandage and showed her how to change the dressing. She would have to continue wearing a protective bandage for a while. Rhoda was determined to stay inside as much as possible, where she could cry her heart out alone.

When Rhoda did dare peek at the scar, she was horrified. The pit the mole's removal had left in her skin was far bigger than she expected, due to the removal of some tissue around the mole itself. Rhoda didn't even care that the cancer was gone and that the surgery had been a success. All she cared about was how she looked and how that made her feel—scarred, marked, imperfect.

A good friend stopped by and teased Rhoda for being so vain. It only made

Let us accept the truth, even when it alters our views.

Rhoda feel worse. Now she was not only struggling with her self-esteem, she felt guilty as well. Her depression grew even as the scar began to lessen.

Two months passed, and Rhoda had become a hermit of sorts. She had turned down dates with men, family, and friends. It was Rhoda's sister, Jean, who finally knocked some sense into her. Jean urged Rhoda to accompany her to lunch one day with a new friend Jean had met. Rhoda packed on the makeup over her now unbandaged facial scar and reluctantly agreed to go.

When they arrived at the restaurant, Jean led Rhoda over to a table where a lovely woman sat. The woman looked up at Jean with a beaming smile and then turned her gorgeous green eyes on Rhoda. That's when Rhoda noticed something strange about this new woman, Leslie. She had a glass eye.

Throughout lunch, Rhoda had a hard time not looking at Leslie's glass eye. Yet Leslie didn't seem to care about her eye or

Rhoda's face. In fact, Leslie's infectious charisma and joy for living made Rhoda realize that beauty truly was within. And when two men came over to ask Leslie for her business card, Rhoda felt as though she had come to a turning point.

Leslie and Rhoda became fast friends, and it was Leslie who encouraged Rhoda to go on a date that turned into more than just friendship. It turned into love, but only after Rhoda first learned to face forward and embrace herself and her life.

Dear God, no one understands my suffering, but you do, for you know my heart even better than I do. Help me to walk through this dark valley of my pain and guide me back to the light of truth. I know that I am precious, but I don't feel that way right now. Help me to see the reality of who I am—the magnificent creation you intended me to be. Amen.

Your wounds I will heal, says the Lord.

Jeremiah 30:17

Heavenly Father, you say that you will heal me. Please help me to realize there are different forms of healing. While your healing is sometimes miraculous and other times almost common and everyday, your healing is on occasion invisible. These are moments when life doesn't seem to change, and I have to look inside to find a place of acceptance. It is in this place where I am reminded that who I am is separate from the pain that invades my life. Please help me to turn my thoughts to you. Amen.

*There are no hopeless situations;
there are only men who have grown
hopeless about them.*

Clare Boothe Luce

*Lord, please give us hope. Please help us to put
our trust in you. Amen.*

**We are more likely to be healed if we are
open to the possibility of God making a
difference in our lives.**

YOU MUSTN'T QUIT

When things go wrong, as they sometimes
   will,
When the road you're trudging seems all
   uphill,
When the funds are low and the debts are
   high
And you want to smile, but you have to
   sigh,
When care is pressing you down a bit,
Rest! if you must—but never quit.
Life is queer, with its twists and turns,
As every one of us sometimes learns,
And many a failure turns about
When he might have won if he'd stuck
   it out;
Stick to your task, though the pace seems
   slow—
You may succeed with one more blow.
Success is failure turned inside out—

The silver tint of the clouds of doubt—
And you never can tell how close you are,
It may be near when it seems afar;
So stick to the fight when you're hardest
    hit—
It's when things seem worst that you
    mustn't quit.

author unknown

*As the one perfect, loving Father, He
welcomes our coming to Him—even spilling
out our tears, our sorrow, or our heartache.
Bring it all into His presence. He not only
will accept your heart cry, He will
comfort you.*

Jack Hayford, *I'll Hold You in Heaven*

*Lord, I come to you boldly and gladly. Accept
me as your child, and meet my needs. Amen.*

CLEANING FOR SOPHIE

An acquaintance of Clara's found out that his wife, Sophie, had just been given three weeks to live. Clara wanted to do something to help.

Some people donated money, while others gave their time. Clara heard about a crew that went to the family's house every week to clean, so she volunteered to do that. Eventually her shift came up. She was a little uneasy about going into the home of someone she didn't know well and cleaning it, especially under the circumstances. Would the family be uncomfortable with her there? It's hard enough to know what to say to a loved one who is ill, let alone someone you hardly know.

The crew arrived at 8:30 A.M. on a cold, cloudy Saturday. They each worked in a different room; Clara focused on the kitchen. The children and husband were helpful and talkative. "Sophie was so sick, we were up most of the night," her husband explained. Clara did not know what to do or say, so she cleaned faster.

After checking to see how everyone else was doing, Clara returned to the kitchen and found Sophie sitting at the table. At first Clara was surprised and not sure what to say. She thought it might be best if she just hurried out of there.

"Would you like some coffee?" Sophie asked.

"Oh, sure," Clara said, hesitantly.

Sophie's warm eyes were comforting, but there was a deep pain behind them. Sophie and Clara started to talk, and the conversation flowed naturally and easily. They touched on a variety of topics: everything from holiday traditions to their kids' reluctance to do their homework. They also

God is love, and those who abide in love abide in God, and God abides in them. Love has been perfected among us in this: that we may have boldness on the day of judgment, because as he is, so are we in this world.

1 John 4:16–17

discussed more serious topics. Sophie said she was proud she had beaten the time frame the doctors had given her. She'd been told she had three weeks to live, which meant she should have passed away in August. But it was now mid-November, and Thanksgiving was just around the corner.

Talking with Sophie made Clara realize that people in any situation just want to be cared for, to be accepted as they are, and to feel a presence of warmth and love. Clara was glad she hadn't been afraid to sit down and talk with Sophie. If she were in that situation, Clara would want the people around her to laugh with her, comfort her, and just spend time with her.

Clara left Sophie's house that morning not only with a thank you and a hug, but with the knowledge that she had helped someone in need. But, in a way, it felt like Sophie had helped Clara more than she'd helped her. Sophie had reminded Clara that everyone, regardless of their circumstances, needs to be acknowledged and loved. It made Clara sad to think how embarrassed she often was to let the people in her life know how much she loves and cares about them. Clara decided to start living each day as if it could be her last and to make reaching out to others a top priority.

A few days later, Clara received a thank-you card from Sophie. "You are one of God's angels," she wrote. "Your unconditional kindness is a great example for others."

Clara went back to clean again a few weeks later and learned that Sophie was in the hospital. While the crew was cleaning, Sophie's husband got a call to come pick her up. She was doing well enough to come home and spend Christmas with her family.

By the new year, Sophie was very weak. She slipped into an unconscious state and was taken to the hospital, where she spent several days. The group that was scheduled to clean her house next called her hospital room to see how she was doing and spoke with her husband. Fifteen minutes after that phone call, Sophie went home to be with God.

Clara thanked God for bringing Sophie into her life. Sophie would always have a special place in Clara's heart. Even when Sophie's body was ailing, her faithfulness, her strength, and her joyful soul were an inspiration to everyone who met her. She taught Clara about loving and living and how to be a more caring person. In her memory and her honor, Clara would try to be a little more kind, a little more helpful, and a little more loving every day.

God Almighty, thank you for the people that inspire me to accept others. Let me learn to love everyone—including myself. Amen.

Discovering Joy

*Don't postpone joy. Even in the
midst of the storm, the flower grows.*

Guide my footsteps, Lord,
To that blessed place
Where pain and sorrow are washed away
Under the sunshine of your love.

**God's love brightens and beautifies even the
darkest days.**

God hath not promised
Skies always blue,
Flower-strewn pathways
All our lives through;
God hath not promised
Sun without rain,
Joy without sorrow,
Peace without pain.
But God hath promised
Strength for the day,
Rest for the labor,
Light for the way,
Grace for the trials,
Help from above,
Unfailing sympathy,
Undying love.

Annie Johnson Flint

A DAWNING

It had been a long, hard early morning struggle among Stephanie's mind, heart, soul, and various achy body parts, but she finally pulled on her shirt, shorts, and running shoes and headed reluctantly out the door for a run. *Just two miles this morning,* Stephanie thought. *I'll just go down to the park and back. It shouldn't take more than 20 minutes.*

The April air was cold and damp, matching her mood. The sun was pouting behind a suspicious-looking gray cloud. *What am I doing out here?* Stephanie wondered. *I could have slept two more hours. My back hurts. There's a nagging ache in my heel.*

As she trudged down the block and turned the corner, Stephanie seriously considered giving up and walking back home. *Who cares? What does it matter?* She grouched silently at God for making her life so miserable. The pavement felt hard and unforgiving under her feet. She clenched her hands tightly, feeling the arthritis grabbing at every joint.

Stephanie's mind drifted over the death of her dad, only a year ago, and on to her mom, alone and lonely at 80 after 60 years of marriage. She thought about her own divorce, still a fresh wound in her heart, and then about her youngest son, who inherited the alcoholism gene from both her family and that of her ex-husband.

Each sunrise reveals a new opportunity to experience joy.

What's the point of it all? Who would even know if I crawled back under the covers and pulled a blanket over my face?

She turned the corner and stopped in her tracks. A wheelchair blocked the way. The brake was set, and it was empty. A hundred steps down the sidewalk a white-haired man, bent and wobbly, carefully put one foot in front of the other, all the while holding tightly to the wrought-iron fence.

He turned to look at Stephanie, and his leathery face crinkled into a smile. "Morning," he said. "Isn't this a beautiful day?"

Stephanie froze in place, staring into his marvelously lined and wrinkled face. She could see the pain behind his eyes, the determination, the truth that this is indeed a beautiful day. He was proof, alive and walking.

The sun peeked out behind them, seemingly as uncertain as Stephanie's frame of mind. Her shadow stretched out in front of her, dark and motionless.

An ocean wave of understanding curled over her, washing across her face and her eyes. She felt like the blind man clutching Jesus' robe. Her eyes were open. She saw.

Stephanie saw her dad dying with a merciful swiftness from a heart attack before the bone cancer settled in to cause him unrelenting agony. She saw her mom surrounded by a wealth of loving friends. She saw her mother playing golf—*walking* 18 holes of golf—three days a week, healthy and well. Although the future was still uncertain for her ex-husband and her, she saw how they talked to each other now as friends and adults, not as spoiled children who must each have his or her own way. And her son . . . she saw her beautiful son, who had been clean and sober from drugs and alcohol for almost two years.

She felt the sun on her back like a soft, warm blanket, and the urge to pull it over her head and disappear from the world was fading from her heart.

"Yes," Stephanie said to the gentleman who was politely waiting for her reply. "It's a fantastic day." His smile was as warm and bright as the morning.

Stephanie moved on, watching him make his way down the length of the iron fence, then turn around and start back.

After a moment, she stepped into a jog again, trying to decide how to thank God for the gentle reminder that this was indeed the day he had made for her.

It was easy. She turned left at the next corner—away from home—and headed out for her long course, wondering at the softness of the pavement under her feet.

God, shine your healing light down upon me today, for my path is filled with painful obstacles and my suffering fogs my vision. Clear the challenges from the road I must walk upon, or at least walk with me as I confront them. With you, I know I can endure anything. With you, I know I can make it through to the other side, where joy awaits. Amen.

My brothers and sisters, whenever you face trials of any kind, consider it nothing but joy, because you know that the testing of your faith produces endurance; and let endurance have its full effect, so that you may be mature and complete, lacking in nothing.

James 1:2–4

Joy is not gush; joy is not jolliness. Joy is perfect acquiescence in God's will because the soul delights in God himself.

H. W. Webb-Peploe

Dear God, we trust you to show us joy when the time comes. We know that good follows bad. Please help us to be patient. Amen.

You show me the path of life. In your presence there is fullness of joy; in your right hand are pleasures forevermore.

Psalm 16:11

The root of faith produces the flower of heart-joy. We may not at first rejoice, but it comes in due time. We trust the Lord when we are sad, and in due season He so answers our confidence that our faith turns to fruition and we rejoice in the Lord. Doubt breeds distress, but trust means joy in the long run.

Charles Spurgeon, *Faith's Checkbook*

Whate'er my fears or foes suggest,
you are my hope, my joy, my rest.
My heart shall feel your love and raise
my cheerful voice to sing your praise.

Isaac Watts

Open up my heavy heart,
That surely day by day,
The bitterness and wrath in me
Will slowly drain away.
God let your spirit enter in
And fill each empty space
With peace and healing to my soul
Through your unending grace.

But for you who revere my name the sun of
righteousness shall rise, with healing
in its wings.

Malachi 4:2

FULL CIRCLE

It had been 25 years since Michelle last spent Christmas with her father. The memories had washed away over the years, and now a lifetime and a generation later he was there to spend the holidays with Michelle's own family. She looked forward to it with childlike anticipation.

His Christmas stocking hung on the mantel with the other family stockings, the name *Papa* at the top, and Michelle looked at it with pride. Her dad would be with her family for Christmas. Their roles reversed, she couldn't wait to see his face, watching his grandchildren on their first Christmas morning together. Michelle happily shopped for and wrapped his presents, excitement growing each day as it got closer to Christmas.

He stayed with them for a week, and it was a time of them getting to know him and he them. They filled their days with baking and holiday music. Michelle's father and her husband got to know each other as they worked on projects around the house. Michelle thought it wonderful to hear them working together: hammering, painting, and learning about family.

Each night her father joined them in prayer. Michelle knew he had no one to pray with, and she often saw tears slip down his cheeks as he felt the love in their home. How the years of being alone must have taken their toll! He hadn't known what it meant to be a complete family for decades, and Michelle began to imagine for the first time what that must have been like for him.

The Lord has done great things for us, and we are filled with joy. Restore our fortunes, O Lord.

Psalm 126:3–4 NIV

He took Michelle's teenage son for walks, their relationship bonding in the crisp, frosty air amid the street lamps and snow flurries. He spent time coloring with her daughter, discussing the meaning of life as they tried to stay between the lines. Michelle's youngest played trains with him, and occasionally she had to break up an argument over whose turn it was to drive the train. They wrestled and laughed, and Michelle watched her father grow from the time he spent with her children.

They all sang Christmas carols together, his beautiful voice bringing back childhood memories of him playing the guitar with Michelle and her sisters singing along with him. The good nostalgia began to resurface, and Michelle felt an emptiness that she had never realized was there before being filled by her father's presence. Years of being without her dad were now being smoothed away by the new memories they were creating together.

Christmas morning arrived, and Michelle was up before the children, grasping the video camera and waiting for her family to wake up, afraid to miss any of it. Curled up on the couch in the dark, camera in hand, she suddenly remembered a Christmas with her dad. She smiled as the warm thoughts washed over her and for a few moments she was able to relive a memory she had thought was lost forever. Her father's laugh and the squeals from her and her sisters flooded her mind. It was a small moment, frozen in time, but a gift for Michelle, nevertheless.

The children and her father finally woke up and joined her. Handing the camera to her husband, Michelle gave her dad his Christmas stocking, crammed with surprises. "Merry Christmas, Daddy." Tears made their way down her father's face, and he held her tighter than he ever had. Through the tears, he whispered, "Merry Christmas, honey. I love you."

The house filled with the beautiful sounds of a Christmas morning that Michelle would never forget. She would forever hold the memory in her heart. She knew they had come full circle, and she had been given a gift she had waited a quarter of a century to receive. They were a family again.

Heavenly Father, we are thankful for family.
Please bring our family together in happiness.
Help us to see everything as your children do:
with wonder and awe. Glorious are your
creations! Thank you for creating us. We love
our family. We love you. Amen.

Pray your way to healing.
Hope your way to courage.
Faith your way to wisdom.
Love your way to joy.

Lord, bless all those today who need healing of any kind. Whether it be physical, emotional, or mental, bless them with your merciful grace and eternal love. Let each one know that they are special in your eyes and that, in the realm of spirit, there is only perfection, wholeness, and joy. Amen.

Healing is the soul expressing the joy of being whole.

Heal me, O Lord, and I shall be healed; save me, and I shall be saved; for you are my praise.

Jeremiah 17:14

Blessed Father, when we think of joy, we often think of things that are new—a new day, a new baby, a new love, a new beginning, the promise of a new home with you in heaven. Rejoicing in these things originates with having joy in you who make all things new. Rather than relying on earthly pleasures to provide happiness, the Scriptures command that we rejoice in you and in each new day you bring. Joy is a celebration of the heart that goes beyond circumstances to the very foundation of joy—the knowledge that we are loved by you. Help us to rejoice in your teachings. Amen.

FALLING TOGETHER

The *D* word scared Amanda in a way that nothing else did. After 15 years of marriage, she and her husband, Jeff, were getting a divorce, and the thought of being alone after all that time terrified her.

She and Jeff had been drifting apart for several years but had always been able to brush their problems under the rug for the sake of their two young children. But now the problems between them were getting so bad, they could not help but argue in front of the kids. They knew it was time to break away, for their own sanity and for the sanity of their children.

It was agreed that Amanda would have custody of the kids during the week, with Jeff taking them for most weekends. They tried to be adults and keep the divorce as amicable as possible, but it was inevitable that things would come up. The entire process wore down Amanda to the point that she ended up in the hospital for three days with severe stomach problems. Her doctor was sure it was caused by stress.

Those three days were grueling, as she had to call her mother to come and watch the kids. Amanda knew Jeff would be telling others how unreliable she was, and it broke her heart. She had wanted to keep things civil, but now she was beginning to see a side of Jeff she had never seen or perhaps she had denied in order to keep the peace.

On the third day of her stay, Amanda could not stop crying. She suffered a breakdown in her

Hope is the joyful liberation of the heart from the darkest prison of despair.

bed, alone but for a nurse attending her, and had to be sedated. Everything was falling apart, and she simply could not take it anymore.

The three-day stay extended to five, so Amanda's doctor could keep watch over her. Amanda knew it was sort of a "suicide watch," but she had no intention of killing herself. She could not do that to her children. Now that they had no real family anymore, leaving them without a mom would destroy them.

Amanda couldn't do much more than lie in bed and watch TV, and the drugs made her head foggy. But when she got tired of watching soap operas and game shows, she began to close her eyes and pray quietly for peace, hope, and guidance on what to do next. Then she meditated so she could listen for her inner spirit's voice. It had been so long since she even acknowledged it; she wanted to be totally aware when it did speak.

She began to get a very distinct feeling of joy. She thought it was the drugs, but the joy persisted on a level deeper than she had ever known before. She also felt a sense of certainty that she had done the right thing and that all would be well. Again, she had no reason to believe this from outer appearances, but she remembered that faith was evidence of things unseen, as the Bible had said.

When her mom brought her two girls to visit, they were surprised to see Amanda smiling. Her face held a resolve she had not felt in years. Clearly her daughters were affected by it and ran to their mom and smothered her in kisses.

Amanda went home the next day with her doctor's blessing. She felt strong, determined, and even excited about what life had in store. She had not fallen apart. She had fallen together.

Lord, help me to understand that the challenges I am going through serve to empower me. Teach me the wisdom to discern that my trials mold me into something far grander than even I could have imagined. Amen.

Then the eyes of the blind shall be opened, and the ears of the deaf unstopped; then the lame shall leap like a deer, and the tongue of the speechless sing for joy.

Isaiah 35:5–6

When we awake the sleeping lion of potential within, we allow it to spring forth in our lives with a mighty, joyful roar.

Joyful is the one who, having been healed, also learns to go forth and heal others.

O Holy Creator, who hath bound together heaven and earth, let me walk through your kingdom comforted and protected by the warm rays of your love. Let me be healed as I stand basking in the divine light of your presence, where strength, hope, and joy are found. Let me sit at rest in the valley of your peace, surrounded by the fortress of your loving care. Amen.

You will go out in joy and be led forth in peace; the mountains and hills will burst into song before you.

Isaiah 55:12 NIV

Surprising Opportunities

*My trust is in you, God of miracles
and surprises, for I feel your presence
in so many ways.*

AN OPPORTUNITY TO HEAL

She is fighting cancer. "Her cancer," as
she refers to it, is a brain tumor. It is slowly
turning her world inside out, short-
circuiting her body's normal abilities and
changing her life forever. However, the
changes to her spirit—the changes that
really count—are inspiring.

Hospitalized yet again, Carrie is determined to make a difference to the other
patients on her floor. She asked her family
for a special present, and they obliged,

returning to the hospital with bundles of flowers to grant Carrie's wish.

Her sister, Jennifer, looks down at the bouquet of red roses in her arms and reflects how often Carrie takes gifts given to her to people she thinks needs them more. Jennifer's eyes burn with held-in tears as she thinks of Carrie, fighting to make her way to brighten the days of the other patients. Carrie's right side is paralyzed by the tumor, and she needs a nurse or one of her family members to help her.

Undaunted by the obstacles, Carrie strives to ease the suffering around her. Her cancer has not made her needy or self-centered but rather the opposite. She sees only other people's needs. Carrie immerses herself in the task of helping others.

Carrie understands everything the other patients are going through because she is going through it too. Only for Carrie, it . has become a blessing. She actually thanks God in her prayers for this opportunity. That is what she calls it: "an opportunity."

It has taught her selflessness and compassion, and Jennifer has watched it help Carrie reach her greatest potential as a human being.

And so Carrie gives. If someone brings her a ceramic angel, it disappears. It might be seen again when peeking into another patient's room. If someone brings her a teddy bear, it finds its way into the arms of the elderly cancer patient next door who loves bears. The gifts her visitors bring are selflessly given to someone else whose pain can be banished if even for a moment with her help. Carrie's smile lights up the room, and the instant the other patients see her, they feel the warmth of her love and her genuine compassion.

Arriving on her floor, Jennifer quickly brushes the tears away and forces her brightest smile for Carrie. Jennifer strides into Carrie's room with her special request and lays the roses on Carrie's bed, where Carrie anxiously waits. Grinning into Carrie's eyes, the exact same shade as Jennifer's, Jennifer helps Carrie into the wheelchair and lays the vivid red roses in her lap. Jennifer watches in wonder as Carrie carefully separates each individual rose with one "good" hand. They then begin their trek.

Slowly they make their way to every room, and Jennifer watches the faces, full of pain, transform into radiant smiles as they see Carrie. For their few moments with her, they feel the joy of God's love, as pure as sunshine breaking through the clouds. Carrie brings smiles and kindness into each room and leaves behind a lingering spirit of hope.

Carrie is tired, and they finish the visits, leaving each patient not only the roses, but also a sense of being loved and being healed.

> *Healing is a matter of time,*
>
> *But it is sometimes also a matter of opportunity.*
>
> Hippocrates

Lord, although we are often not certain of your intentions when you present us with unpleasant circumstances, we understand that you do have a reason. The hurt isn't just to spite us. Please help us to keep our outlooks positive and allow us to aid others who are as dismayed and in just as much pain as we are. Amen.

All the paths of the Lord are loving and faithful.

Psalm 25:10

Then the king will say to those at his right hand, "Come, you that are blessed by my Father, inherit the kingdom prepared for you . . . for I was hungry and you gave me food, I was thirsty and you gave me something to drink, I was a stranger and you welcomed me, . . . I was sick and you took care of me."

Matthew 25:34–36

Father, help us to touch and influence others. We want them to recognize and celebrate even the small blessings. We want to surprise them with gestures of love. Amen.

Thank heaven for summer rain!
Through the pall of the sweltering sky,
It falls like kisses to the earth,
Renewing and nourishing.
Like a child
I run—
Arms open,
Face to the clouds,
Into the downpour.
All around the people hide
Under doorways and umbrellas,
While the rain pours down on me,
Washing away my gloom.

Faith does not fear change, but knows that all change is simply the spirit's way of moving our life in the direction of our destiny.

O welcome pure-ey'd Faith, white-handed
   Hope,
Thou hovering angel girt with golden
   wings...
I see you visibly and now believe
That he, the Supreme good...
Would send a glistening Guardian if need
   were
To keep my life and honor unassailed.

John Milton

*God is our refuge and strength, a very
present help in trouble. Therefore we will
not fear, though the earth should change,
though the mountains shake in the heart of
the sea; though its waters roar and foam,
though the mountains tremble with its
tumult. The Lord of hosts is with us.*

Psalm 46:1–3, 7

The resilient heart withstands the winds of change, just as the flexible branch of a tree bends but does not break.

Father, you will help us to survive the seasons of surprises in our lives. For just as the harshest winter always gives way to the warm blush of spring, the season of our suffering will give way to a brighter tomorrow, where change becomes a catalyst for new growth and spiritual maturity. Amen.

If we don't change, we don't grow. If we don't grow, we are not really living.

Gail Sheehy

ALONE TIME

Karen couldn't understand why it had hit her so hard. After all, she was ready—actually more than ready these last few contentious months—to have her daughter, Rebecca, leave home for college. And yet after she left Rebecca's dorm room, both of them blinking back tears and promising to e-mail as soon as Rebecca was hooked up, Karen sobbed all three hours of the trip back home.

It turned out that was only a drop in the vast ocean of her tears. *It's a natural passage,* she told herself. *It's a relief not to have any more squabbles about curfews,* she told herself. *Rebecca's adjusting beautifully,* she told herself. And then she asked herself, *So why have I been crying every day for the last three weeks?*

Karen's husband, Bill, was the one who suggested she take a trip, maybe go someplace warm with a friend and sip big, silly mixed drinks with coconut juice and parasols in them. It was the peak of Bill's busy season at work, or he would have joined her.

Karen was touched by his generosity and concern. When she thought it over, though, she realized that besides the fact that she wasn't fit company, she actually wanted to be alone. In fact, upon reflection, it dawned on her that she had gone directly from the home of her father to the home of her husband and then immediately had a child. Besides, a bright and sunny vacation place with the throbbing of steel drums in the background and the bright clothes of wealthy vacationers did not fit her mood.

A small thing, as simple as a breath of fresh air, supports the changes we make: The present is breathing in, and the past is exhalation.

She wanted a subtler landscape, a place as sober as she felt. And so it was that to the astonishment of her friends, her family, and most of all herself, Karen found herself staying alone for a week in a rustic cabin at a state park in the sandhills of

Nebraska. She didn't pack any makeup or a curling iron, and she took off her watch as soon as she arrived. She soon found that she wasn't truly alone. During a long, healing nap, for example, she dreamed about Rebecca as a dimpled toddler instead of the willowy young woman she had become. She thought about Bill as he was when she first knew him, her parents before they'd gone gray, her grandparents, her childhood friends, and her younger self—and what that had all meant and means in her life.

The stack of books she had brought remained unread; the CDs unplayed in the battery-operated CD player. She sat in a chair in the fire ring outside her cabin and watched the sun come up in the morning and the sun go down at night. It didn't worry her that she was unable to put words to her feelings and prayers because she began to understand that sometimes the God she believed in could only be found in the silence beyond language. She began to see Nebraska not as a place to roar through on the interstate on the way to someplace else but as a dramatic backdrop for the thunderstorms she watched from her bed in the cabin at night, the lightning stark and jagged. She listened to the music of the wind in the pine trees nearby. The rhythms of her day were determined by a hike up and down the sandhills in the morning and a fire at night.

By the end of her week, Karen was still leaking a little with tears, when she thought about her daughter no longer living at home. The good part was that she no longer berated herself for crying; after all, Rebecca had been her lifework for 18 years, and the sudden rupture was painful. It would take a while to heal. Her summing up had led her to understand that while perhaps she hadn't been a perfect mother to Rebecca, she had been more than good enough. She realized that she was pretty good company, all by herself. As she turned in the cabin key and headed home, she found herself singing along with the radio. She could hardly wait to see Bill. She wasn't sure what surprises it would bring, but she was looking forward to Act II.

Thank you, Great Healer, for this second chance at life. Forgive me for being surprised, as if healing were beyond possibility and your intention. Amen.

O Hope! dazzling, radiant Hope!
—What a change thou bringest to the
   hopeless,
brightening the darkened paths,
and cheering the lonely way.

                   Aimee Semple McPherson

Precious Lord, bless me with your grace that I may experience the deepest peace and healing that only you can provide. Show me the merciful love that knows no end that I may rest today knowing I am cared for. Amen.

Jesus went with him, and the crowd thronged behind. In the crowd was a woman who had been sick for twelve years with a hemorrhage. She had suffered much from many doctors through the years and had become poor from paying them, and was no better but, in fact, was worse. She had heard all about the wonderful miracles Jesus did, and that is why she came up behind him through the crowd and touched his clothes. For she thought to herself, "If I can just touch his clothing, I will be healed." And sure enough, as soon as she had touched him,

the bleeding stopped and she knew she was well! Jesus realized at once that healing power had gone out from him, so he turned around in the crowd and asked, "Who touched my clothes?"... Then the frightened woman, trembling at the realization of what had happened to her, came and fell at his feet and told him what she had done. And he said to her, "Daughter, your faith has made you well; go in peace, healed of your disease."

Mark 5:24–34 TLB

Only by moving through the pain do we get to embrace the gift of healing and call it our own.

LUCKY BREAK

Loren had trained for nine months for the upcoming 10-mile race. But when she broke her ankle during a training run only three days before, she was certain she was cursed.

All of the time and energy spent getting her body ready for the grueling run went right out the window as the emergency room doctor set her ankle in a cast. She would wear it for weeks, but the depression of not making her goal of crossing that finish line was bound to last far longer.

The day of the race, Loren could not bear to watch it on her local TV station. She instead had her own little pity party, crying over her terrible fate and cursing her clumsiness. When a good friend called to console her, Loren acted like a brat, whining and moaning about how God must hate her for letting this happen to her after all the work she did.

As the day went on, Loren fell asleep and was abruptly awakened by a knock on the door. Sure it was her good friend coming to check on her, she didn't answer, wanting to be alone in her misery. But the knocking persisted, and Loren finally hobbled to the door and opened it.

Her jaw dropped, and a gasp escaped her lips. There, standing before her was her best friend, Tracy,

Those who hope in the Lord will renew their strength.

Isaiah 40:31 NIV

from high school. They had not seen each other in 12 years and had lost touch a while back.

Tracy was so glad Loren was home. She explained that she was only in town for a few hours on a layover and just had to come find her old friend. Loren invited her in, and they spent the next two hours talking and laughing, as if their friendship had never ended. In fact, Loren learned that Tracy, too, loved to run and was planning on doing the Chicago Marathon in a year. Tracy challenged Loren to come to

Chicago, stay with her for a few weeks, and run the marathon with her. The idea delighted Loren, and her spirits soared at the thought of running such a challenging course.

When Tracy did have to go, Loren was sad to say good-bye, but the two promised to keep in touch via e-mail and make Loren's travel plans in about nine months. As she closed the door, Loren realized that had she gone to run, she would have missed Tracy's short visit. She looked up toward heaven and winked, thanking God for the lucky break.

God, thank you for sometimes reminding me that in the center of chaos lies the seed of new opportunity and that things are not always as awful as they seem at first. I often forget that what starts out bad can end up great and that it is all a matter of my own perspective. Amen.

The only real obstacle that stands between pain and healing is our limited mind.

One song can spark a moment,
One flower can wake the dream.
One tree can start a forest,
One bird can herald spring.
One smile begins a friendship,
One hand clasp lifts a soul.
One star can guide a ship at sea,
One word can frame the goal.
One vote can change a nation,
One sunbeam lights a room.
One candle wipes out darkness,
One laugh will conquer gloom.

unknown

Reaching Out

Going through a difficult time alone feels like trying to find your way through a pitch-black room. The moment you reach out to another person, a light appears that guides you to the other side, where the door to healing awaits.

We have but faith: we cannot know;
For knowledge is of things we see;
And yet we trust it comes from thee,
A beam in darkness: let it grow.

Alfred, Lord Tennyson

Lord, you are here,

Lord, you are there.

You are wherever we go.

Lord, you guide us,

Lord, you protect us.

You are wherever we go.

Lord, we need you,

Lord, we trust you,

You are wherever we go.

Lord, we love you,

Lord, we praise you,

You are wherever we go.

chant of the Dinka tribe of the Southern Sudan

The Lord is my strength and my shield; in him my heart trusts; so I am helped, and my heart exults, and with my song I give thanks to him.

Psalm 28:7–8

Listen to this wise advice; follow it closely, for it will do you good, and you can pass it on to others: Trust in the Lord.

Proverbs 22:17–19 TLB

I thank you for the healing power of friends and for the positive emotions friendship brings. Thank you for sending companions to me so we can support and encourage one another and share our joys and sorrows. My friends represent for me your presence and friendship here on earth. Please keep them in your care, Father. We need each other, and we need you. Amen.

I'LL BE THERE

Caring for her elderly mother had begun to take its toll on Cynthia. She had not wanted to put her mom into a nursing home and thought she could give her the round-the-clock attention she needed. But even with no children of her own, a flexible work-at-home job, and her own good health, Cynthia was beginning to feel exhausted.

Her mother had been diagnosed with congestive heart failure and had been in and out of hospitals for the last few months. The elderly woman also suffered from the beginning stages of Alzheimer's and had advanced osteoporosis, which kept her bound to a wheelchair.

Cynthia had watched her once healthy and vibrant mother deteriorate over the last year; it happened so quickly it took her breath away. She was simply not ready to let her mom go and wanted to try to care for her as long as possible.

But her own health was beginning to suffer, and this week marked the third time in two months she'd had a terrible cold. Even her sister, Jean, who lived several states away, was urging Cynthia to find a good nursing home for their mother and offered to help pay for it, too. But Cynthia insisted she could handle it.

The healing presence of God is always working in and through us, but only when we give up the illusion of control.

Then Cynthia's cold turned into bronchitis and then into pneumonia, and Cynthia herself was hospitalized for a few days with her lungs full of fluid.

Her body's immune system could not handle the stress of caring for her mom, and now Cynthia was going into a breakdown mode. Still, all she could worry about was her mom, who was now at Cynthia's Aunt Betty's. Betty was not much healthier than Cynthia's mom, but it was better than leaving her mom alone.

Jean called Cynthia at the hospital. Cynthia began rambling into the phone about their mother. She started crying uncontrollably. Jean tried to console Cynthia. Jean told Cynthia that she was going to catch the next flight into town.

Once Jean arrived, she took over the reins and helped care for Cynthia as well as their mom. When she saw how tired and burnt out Cynthia was, Jean told her that she had been considering moving into town so she could help care for their mom and that she had decided to do it. Cynthia was so relieved, and for once she was willing to give up control. Just knowing someone else would be there to help did more to speed up her own healing than any medicine, and when Jean told their mom she was moving back home, there were tears of sheer joy in the old woman's eyes.

Cynthia didn't know how to thank Jean for her major life decision, but to Cynthia, the only thing that mattered was that they all would be there for each other, healing together with God's help.

God, help me to accept the help I need and to give up my stubborn need to control the outcome of every situation. Show me that sometimes my will is not always the best and that sometimes you send us healing angels in the form of other humans. Thank you. Amen.

Be it ours, when we cannot see the face of God, to trust under the shadow of his wings.

Charles H. Spurgeon

How precious is your steadfast love, O God! All people may take refuge in the shadow of your wings.

Psalm 36:7

And those who know your name put their trust in you, for you, O Lord, have not forsaken those who seek you.

Psalm 9:10

God, why is there so much pain in the world? It's so hard to understand. Help us through it all. Help us to comprehend or at least to simply trust in you. Amen.

Trust in the Lord with all your heart and lean not on your own understanding; in all your ways acknowledge him, and he will make your paths straight.

Proverbs 3:5–6 NIV

O magnify the Lord with me;
with me exalt his name;
when in distress to him I called,
he to my rescue came.
The hosts of God encamp around
the dwellings of the just;
deliverance he affords to all
who in his goodness trust.

Nahum Tate

Have thine own way, Lord! Have thine own way! Wounded and weary, help me I pray! Power, all power, surely is thine! Touch me and heal me, Savior divine!

Adelaide A. Pollard,
"Have Thine Own Way, Lord"

The suffering isn't your fault. God's plan for you can be trusted.

God, I pray to you today for the healing that only you can bring. I long to be free from pain and suffering, to be whole again in body, mind, and spirit. Give to me the soothing balm of your tender, loving care that I might mount up on wings of eagles and fly with ease again. Amen.

Come to me, all you that are weary and are carrying heavy burdens, and I will give you rest. Take my yoke upon you, and learn from me; for I am gentle and humble in heart, and you will find rest for your souls. For my yoke is easy, and my burden is light.

Matthew 11:28–30

Come, ye disconsolate, where'er ye
languish;
Come, at the shrine of God fervently
kneel;
Here bring your wounded hearts; here tell
your anguish;
Earth has no sorrow that heaven cannot
heal.

Thomas Moore, *Sacred Songs*

*Now may our Lord Jesus Christ himself and
God our Father, who loved us and through
grace gave us eternal comfort and hope,
comfort your hearts and strengthen them in
every good work and word.*

2 Thessalonians 2:16–17

NEVER GIVE UP

At 15, Melissa thought she was invincible. It was her sophomore year in high school, and she and her sister Tara were in the school talent show. It was a February night, and practice had run late. Tara's classmate Brad offered them a ride home in his van, and although Melissa didn't know if she liked Brad, she didn't want to walk home in the dark. With an uneasy feeling in the pit of her stomach, Melissa climbed into Brad's van.

When they were near Melissa and Tara's street, Brad began taunting Melissa, calling her names until she had had enough. Melissa told him she wanted to walk the rest of the way home, and he pulled over. Relieved, Melissa got out and started walking the last few houses toward home. Laughing, Brad pretended to run Melissa over, driving up on the sidewalk. Melissa remembered thinking they were almost home and that he was going as slow as she was walking, so she hopped up onto the back of his van and held on to the handle of the back door. Melissa's plan was to just hop back off again when they got to their house.

Suddenly Brad was speeding up, and Melissa saw her house pass by in a blur. She was shaking and yelling at him to stop. Tara was screaming at him, too. Melissa pounded on the door as hard as she could. She couldn't believe he was doing this; she couldn't believe how stupid she was to get on the back of his van. She thought, *I should have trusted my first instinct to not ride with him.* It was dark, and he wasn't stopping. Melissa lost her footing, and suddenly there was all this space below her.

Melissa woke up on the side of the road, and her mother was there, bending over her. Her sister was crying, and there was blood everywhere. She put her hand up to her head, and it was instantly covered with the sticky warmth of her own blood. She tried to sit up and passed out. The next thing she knew she was in the emergency room and the pain was unbelievable. Melissa had a severely fractured skull, diagonally from the top to the bottom of her head, and a massive concussion. She couldn't move without getting sick so she had to stay perfectly still. Her parents and sister were with her, their faces pale and frightened.

Turn over your problems to God, and he will orchestrate the best outcome.

The next several days were a blur of blinding, unending pain. It just never got better, and Melissa thought she couldn't take it anymore. The pain consumed her, and she began to wish to die. Looking over at her mother, Melissa actually told her she wanted to die—the pain was just too much. Immediately Melissa's mother prayed with her, and a peace came over Melissa. Her mother's prayers brought her a calm, comforted feeling, and through them she stopped wanting to die and started wanting to get better. Melissa knew she was lucky to be alive. She would sleep a lot, but whenever she woke up, her mother was there, and she would drift off to sleep again, always with her mother's prayers drifting alongside Melissa.

Slowly, day by day, Melissa began to heal—not only her injuries but also her spirit. She knew it was because of the prayers and faith of her mother. Her mother had taught her much about faith, and Melissa knew this had saved her life. Without her mother, Melissa thought that she would have simply given up. Her mother had shown Melissa that no matter how hard or painful life can get, never ever give up.

At 15, Melissa learned life is very precious and worth fighting for. Two decades later, she was still grateful for this understanding. It had brought healing countless times over the years and was truly the gift of a lifetime.

Dear God, hear my prayer. I am suffering and in need of your merciful blessings. Please take me into your arms. Give me the courage to keep going through difficult times and the fortitude to move beyond the outer illusions of pain and despair. Only you can heal me, God. In praise and thanks, amen.

Each prayer is a message of faith in God. We are saying, "I trust you; lead me. I believe in you; guide me. I need you; show me." When we offer ourselves openly, he will always answer.

NOT ASKING MUCH

Take this burden from me, Lord,
Free me from this pain.
Let me move with ease and grace
And walk in health again.
Take this yoke upon you, Lord,
And help me toward my goal,
I'm tired of being sick and tired
And long to be made whole.
Release me from my illness
And restore me to my best.
If you can do that for me, Lord,
I'll take care of the rest.

*He heals the brokenhearted, and binds
up their wounds. Great is our Lord, and
abundant in power; his understanding
is beyond measure. The Lord lifts
up the downtrodden.*

Psalm 147:3, 5–6

Father, there are many events in our lives over which we have no control. However, we do have a choice either to endure trying times or to give up. Remind us that the secret of survival is remembering that our hope is in your fairness, goodness, and justice. When we put our trust in you who cannot fail us, we can remain faithful. Our trust and faithfulness produce the endurance that sees us through the tough times we all face in this life. Please help us to remember. Amen.

I believe in some blending of hope and sunshine sweetening the worse lots. I believe that this life is not all; neither the beginning nor the end. I believe while I tremble; I trust while I weep.

Charlotte Brontë

A MATTER OF COURSE

The morning sun clearly defined the mountains, promising a pristine day and beckoning him to answer the call of the links. He had left the house early, but not too early. Not before helping Patricia through the first part of their daily routine.

Not before gently lifting her in and out of the bathtub. Not before shepherding her back to the bedroom. Not before erasing the ravages of another sleepless night by combing her hair into place.

I am weak, but thou art mighty; hold me with thy powerful hand.

William Williams, "Guide Me, O Thou Great Jeremiah"

He wiped the dimpled ball, nestled it on the green of the ninth hole, and picked up his marker. Gazing at the lush grass, he bent his knees and gripped the putter.

Patricia had loved walking the course, listening to the hushed stillness. He could point out the geese gliding on the pond and the fragrant crabapple trees laced with blossoms. A love of outdoors was something they shared.

And they shared a lot. Six daughters. Twenty grandchildren. Allegiance to church. Devotion to each other. That hadn't changed, but other things had.

He lowered his head and hunched his broad shoulders over the extra-long club.

Once Patricia's slender, athletic body had complemented his rugged 6'5" frame. Now crutches supported her stooped shoulders.

Once she had gracefully whirled with him on the dance floor. Now the only spinning she did was a turn through the shopping mall in her wheelchair.

Once her nimble fingers had flown at the sewing machine, tucked a blanket around a slumbering child, and tidied the house. Now, crooked and gnarled, they sat idle in her lap.

Rheumatoid arthritis had invaded their lives only nine years into their marriage. He watched it ravage his wife's body. The changes it made were both immediate and gradual, until—quite clearly—the disease determined their course in life.

He stiffened his wrists. Closing his stance, he shifted his weight forward.

Some people thought he carried quite a load. But as Patricia was able to do less, he simply did more. He merely broadened his definition of husband, the job title he considered most sacred. He added the roles of cook, housekeeper, beautician, and chauffeur—even nurse.

He and Patricia were good together. After all, they had perfected their team-work through 24 surgeries. He knew better than any health care worker how to lift her, turn her, and tend to her personal needs. That last hip replacement came at a high price for them both: a permanent infection that added a new element to their routine. Now his large hands tenderly applied fresh dressings twice daily to the draining wound.

He drew the putter into a slow backward stroke. He completed his putt with a firm follow-through.

He rarely glanced back at their old dreams. Instead, together, they had forged new ones. For instance, they purchased a self-contained motor home so he could assist her in the bathroom, something just not acceptable in public restrooms.

And now they could travel because of the motor home. They could visit their kids. They could attend the important family events most precious to them: baptisms, graduations, weddings, funerals.

He watched the ball roll forward in a gentle arc and rim the cup. He listened to its satisfying drop and "thonk." He made par.

Patricia always said other husbands would have left long ago. She even called him "her good-hearted man." But he liked to remind her that those wedding vows some 45 years past were sincere. It wasn't just that he had promised to stay with his wife forever, no matter what happened to one or both of them. It was that he *wanted* to.

He leaned down and, with his thick fingers, plucked up the ball, brushed it on his pants, and tucked it into his pocket.

There would be other days to golf. It was time to go home. Time to fix lunch. Time to help Patricia.

Lord, thank you for bringing others into our lives to help us heal. We appreciate how much they aid us. Please remind us to thank them for reaching out to us. Thank you for extending your love to us through them. Amen.

I believe, God, that you give us faith as a means of getting in touch with your love. For once we have that love, we can pass it on to others.

Henry Drummond, *The Greatest Thing in the World*

For I am convinced that nothing can ever separate us from his love. Death can't, and life can't. The angels won't, and all the powers of hell itself cannot keep God's love away. Our fears for today, our worries about tomorrow, or where we are—high above the sky, or in the deepest ocean—nothing will ever be able to separate us from the love of God demonstrated by our Lord Jesus Christ when he died for us.

Romans 8:38–39 TLB

Your love, God, is always reaching out to us, which is cause for celebration. We want to rejoice in your love every day.

Rejoice in hope, be patient in suffering,
persevere in prayer.

Romans 12:12

God, it's so hard to see your will in suffering.
But while I can't understand your ways, I
trust your heart. And so I cling to the faith
that has sustained me through so many
heartaches before, knowing that although it
may be all I have, it's also all I need. Amen.

If your body suffers pain, and your health
you can't regain, and your soul is almost
sinking in despair, Jesus knows the pain you
feel, he can save and he can heal, take your
burden to the Lord and leave it there.

Charles Albert Tindley

Expressing Feelings

Tell God and others how you feel, because if you voice your pain, it can be whisked away in the wind.

Creator God, you have come to me with healing in your hand. When I cried out, you heard me. You provided me with a gift that brought both peace and pleasure to my harried life. You helped me to focus on life instead of illness and sorrow. Lord, thank you for this wondrous gift. Amen.

In the same way that a small child cannot draw a bad picture, so a child of God cannot offer a bad prayer. So we are brought to the most basic, the most primary form of prayer: Simple Prayer. Let me describe it for you. In Simple Prayer we bring ourselves before God just as we are, warts and all. Like children before a loving father, we open our hearts and make our requests. We do not try to sort things out, the good from the bad. We simply and unpretentiously share our concerns and make our petitions. We tell God, for example, how frustrated we are with the coworkers at the office or the neighbor down the street. We ask for food, favorable weather, and good health.

Richard J. Foster, *Prayer: Finding the Heart's True Home*

REMEDY

Holly's relationship with her daughter Dana couldn't be any worse. Dana was now a teenager, 17, and a real know-it-all. Holly remembered those feelings of invincibility and certainty, and she also remembered all the lousy life lessons she was taught between what she thought she knew and what was really true! She didn't want her daughter to suffer through those same lessons, yet it seemed as though Dana's life was on a path of its own, a path Holly had no control over.

There had been times when Holly cracked the whip of discipline, and that had only angered Dana further. Other times Holly and her husband, Jim, tried to be diplomatic, but that made Dana think she could get away with even more.

Now Dana was threatening to move in with her 19-year-old boyfriend, and Holly was dumbfounded as to how to stop her. She supposed she could put up bars on the doors and windows, but Holly so wanted to get through to Dana without using such tactics. She and Jim had tried talking, reasoning, punishing, grounding, even therapy, but to no avail.

One night, Dana and Holly got into an intense argument while Jim was still at work. Dana got so angry she grabbed some of her clothes and smashed them into a suitcase. She left the house, saying she would be at her boyfriend's and she would return later to retrieve the rest of her stuff.

Holly felt defeated. She sat, slumped and sobbing, at the kitchen table. She decided to pray to God for a new solution to bring her family back together. She prayed that God would take over for there was nothing more she could do. She had no idea her prayers would be answered so quickly. They were—and not at all in the way she had hoped.

Dana called about two hours after she had defiantly took off and begged her mother in tears to come get her. She was at a coffeehouse where her supposed boyfriend had dumped her after an argument in the car. Holly called Jim at work, and he agreed to meet them at the café.

When Holly arrived, Jim hadn't gotten there yet. Dana sat in a corner booth, looking down, her cheeks wet, and slowly swirling the spoon in her coffee. Holly sidled up beside her and put her hand on Dana's shoulder. Without a word, Dana fell into her mom's arms, complaining bitterly about how stupid she was.

> *For there is nothing hidden, except to be disclosed; nor is anything secret, except to come to light. Let anyone with ears to hear listen!*
>
> Mark 4:22–23

Holly could have agreed with Dana and pulled an "I-TOLD-YOU-SO" followed by a condescending lecture on how parents always know better, but instead she just sat quietly and let Dana cry, talk, and express her fears, her hopes, and her anger. It was an enlightening hour for Holly, who spoke not one word. She let Dana unload and learned more about her daughter than she had ever known, and when Jim got there, Holly was confident that they would not have any more problems with Dana's defiant behavior.

Holly had found the remedy to healing the rift between their daughter and themselves. They had learned that sometimes kids just want to be listened to and allowed to make mistakes. As long as Holly and Jim were always there for Dana when she fell, they would remain a strong and loving family.

Lord, look down upon my family with merciful eyes, and help us to heal the divides that threaten to grow between us. Guide us toward the solutions that will empower everyone involved, and remind us that we work better when we work together. Help us to speak honestly with each other. Amen.

Love comforts, never alarms;
Always heals, never harms.
Always grows, never diminishes;
Love begins, never finishes.

Holy God, you have shown me light and life. You are stronger than any natural power. Accept the words from my heart that struggle to reach you. Accept the silent thoughts and feelings that are offered to you. Clear my mind of the clutter of useless facts. Bend down to me, and lift me in your arms. Make me holy as you are holy. Give me a voice to sing of your love to others.

ancient Christian prayer, written on papyrus

A TRADITION OF LOVE

They are smelly and scaly, and Leah hates them. The mere presence of a fish sends her stomach lurching. But fish and fishing are a big part of her life, and strangely enough, she has become grateful for the sport.

Leah has raised her son, now 16, primarily on her own. He has never known his father, and there have been many times in his young life when Leah has prayed hard for that gap in her son's life to be filled. In fact, the pain in that gap has often been more than she could bear.

Leah's brother-in-law is an avid fisherman. Tall, gentle, and quiet, Ken has always included Nick in his fishing trips. Looking back over the past 16 years, Leah realizes this has had more than a casual hand in her son's upbringing. Ken filled the gap so quietly that Leah didn't realize it until there was no gap.

Beginning when Nick was a small boy, Ken would ask to take him fishing. At first Leah balked. Visions of her child tumbling into a rushing river or worse—falling through the ice during a winter ice-fishing trip—gripped her in a panic. But Nick's begging eyes always melted Leah, and she gave in. Every time she waited and prayed for a safe return (and no fish to stink up her house), and every time God answered her prayers in his own way. Leah's enthusiastic, adorable son grew to love fishing over the years and became quite good at it, always

Each life that touches ours for good is a reflection of God's love for us.

bringing the smelly things home and always sporting a happy grin that in a mother's eyes is priceless.

Of course, there were the inevitable slips on the ice, the mishaps of an over-eager boy, scrapes, soggy lunches, frostbite, stuck hooks, and lost poles over the years—all things Leah feared—but all have contributed to a powerful bond between Nick and Ken. As the years have worn on, fishing has become an expected tradition with the two of them. Leah has learned to cope, and although she still prays, she has learned to accept the smell, the muddy clothes, the long days away, and even the fish, because nothing brings as much joy to her son. This tradition of love quietly has healed the gap.

Over time Leah has begun to appreciate that these aren't just fishing trips. They are bonding, talking, silently-thinking-together trips. They are talks about life, family, God, and all that is important in this world. They are golden, laughter-filled days that Nick will long remember and will one day experience with his own children.

Leah's brother-in-law has gently led her son to a path of goodness, of acceptance, and of love. He has taught Nick how to be kind, how to serve, and how to love. Ken has shown Nick, through his humble example, what it means to be a father. This, Leah realizes, is an incredible gift and one that Leah cannot give him.

Leah knows that these trips have brought blessings beyond her recognition, and the mere thought is balm to her spirit. She has seen her son grow into a wonderful, kind, caring young man, and she knows her brother-in-law has had no small part in this. His filling in the gap has also healed the gap. This is the greatest of gifts and one for which Leah will forever be grateful: a tradition of love.

Blessed Creator, thank you for the loving people in my life. Thank you for their open hearts and minds. Thank you for making them like you. Amen.

Create opportunities to express your love and appreciation on a regular basis.

MIGHTY FORTRESS

You are the mighty wind
that lifts me up on high
when I am weak and weary
and without the strength to fly.
You are the mighty fortress
that keeps me free from fear
and shelters me in kindness
with your tender, loving care.

When men are animated by the love of
Christ they feel united, and the needs,
sufferings and joys of others are felt
as their own.

Pope John XXIII

Heal us, Emmanuel, hear our prayer; we wait to feel thy touch; deep-wounded souls to thee repair, and Savior, we are such.

William Cowper, "Heal Us, Emmanuel, Hear Our Prayer"

THE HEALING TOUCH

The light that shines upon me,

The arms that reach to hold me,

The warmth that gives me comfort,

The angel's wings enfold me.

The word that gives me power,

The song that makes me whole,

The wisdom that empowers me,

The touch that heals my soul.

If I have faith it is possible.
Faith knowing God loves and cares—
That all my burdens and trials
He also feels and shares.

In the same way, the Spirit helps us in our weakness. We do not know what we ought to pray for, but the Spirit himself intercedes for us with groans that words cannot express. And he who searches our hearts knows the mind of the Spirit, because the Spirit intercedes for the saints in accordance with God's will.

Romans 8:26–27 NIV

Hear my cry, O God; listen to my prayer. From the end of the earth I call to you, when my heart is faint. Lead me to the rock that is higher than I; for you are my refuge, a strong tower against the enemy.

Psalm 61:1–3

God, keep me close today. I am not at my best, and I would like someone to listen as I whine, moan, and complain. Please bear the brunt of my troubles or send someone to help in your name. Amen.

GIRL TALK

Annette and Claire were only 24 hours into their 72-hour conversation when the voice of Annette's six-year-old—dawdling his way to bedtime—drifted down the stairs: "Are you still talking?"

"Of course!" they answered. By the end of their long "girls' weekend," they were both hoarse. Having been friends who had seen each other through infertility problems, a difficult childbirth, troubled relationships with stepchildren, and at least a dozen diets, both of them grieved when Annette moved clear across the country for her husband's job.

They talked on the phone and e-mailed, but it wasn't as healing as this: sitting in their pajamas with endless cups of tea, with hours to let the conversation roam. After all, a number of major life events had transpired since Annette's move: Annette had coaxed Grandpop into a retirement home, Claire's father had died, Annette's son had started his first year of school, Claire's daughter had married, and

Annette's husband had lost the job for which he had moved in the first place. But even without those topics to explore, the women would not have drained the well of the healing waters of female conversation. They were both that thirsty for it. Claire, who had been a history major in college, told Annette her theory: Like water, most women need girl talk every day.

No matter how alone you feel, you'll find your journey is a shared one.

Maybe the reason that so many women pioneers went mad is not because the locusts ravaged their crops or their babies died, but because as the wind shrieked around the soddies, they had no women friends with whom to talk these tragedies through.

Annette told Claire that when she was a little girl, she used to wonder why her mother and her mother's best friend needed to talk every day. Strangling herself with the phone cord and pestering for soda, Annette would eavesdrop while they covered the same evergreen topics: Fred's migraines, Johnny's bed-wetting, recipes calling for lime gelatin dessert, and the sales at the department store.

Annette's memories of her mother's all-inclusive phone conversations made her realize that she and Claire had almost forgotten to discuss their husbands.

This fact reminded Annette that when her sister had visited recently, the sisters shared a double bed and Annette's husband got the couch. In the morning, they asked him how he'd slept. Annette was touched to hear him say that the couch was fine, and that although he had not been able to hear what they were saying, he had listened into the wee hours to the soft harmony of the women's words and laughter.

"I guess the guys don't want in on our girl talk anyway," Claire told Annette. The two agreed that not many men think it fun to sit together jabbering about feelings for hours. Sure, the men talked about their feelings a little when they lifted weights, cheered for touchdowns, and hung drywall together, but most often their husbands expressed their feelings to their wives because their wives would pry. But no matter because Annette and Claire appreciated that their husbands never begrudged the girlfriends' need for talk.

Annette and Claire were also thankful to God for their friendship. They were happy that his healing power could flow through them. Because of him, they could talk and listen to each other's problems.

"Isn't it wonderful?" Annette asked Claire. "Girl talk is the one form of therapy every woman can afford."

Heavenly Father, I am glad to have even just one companion, but you have sent me many more! I thank you for my friends and family. I am happy to have so many shoulders on which I can lean. Amen.

Rejoice when I run into problems?
Know trials are good for me?
Things like that aren't easy—
Learning to live patiently.

Growing in grace is a process.
Developing character hurts.
Becoming more Christ-like in all things
Is an everyday process called work.

But if I have faith it is possible.
Faith knowing God loves and cares—
That all my burdens and trials
He also feels and shares.

Hope is the best possession. None are completely wretched but those who are without hope.

William Hazlitt

Dear God, it's not fair. It's hard for me to believe that whatever happens is okay. I want to feel your presence, even if you don't offer a miracle. Please understand how I feel and give me hope. Amen.

Hope is a strange invention—
A Patent of the Heart—
In unremitting action
Yet never wearing out.

Emily Dickinson

Comfort, dear God, those whose eyes are filled with tears and those whose backs are near breaking with the weight of a heavy burden. Heal those whose hearts hold a wound and whose faith has been dealt a blow. Bless all who mourn and who despair. Help those who can't imagine how they'll make it through another day. For your goodness and mercy are enough for all the troubles in the world. Amen.

When you are in the dark, listen, and God will give you a very precious message for someone else when you get into the light.

Oswald Chambers

Finding Forgiveness

Be kind to one another, tenderhearted, forgiving one another, as God in Christ has forgiven you.

Ephesians 4:32

Heavenly Father, I ask for your healing presence. Protect me from the worldly hurts and evil that have clouded my life and robbed me of joy. Help me to forget the past, to let go of grudges, and to make a new start. Take away the darkness of my sorrow, and flood it with the light of your love. Forgive me, so I might forgive others. Amen.

PEACEMAKING

The day Leslie and Tom moved into their new house, they sensed a potential problem with an older male neighbor who seemed hell-bent on criticizing everything. First, it was where the moving truck was parked, then it was a box that tumbled accidentally into his yard, and by day's end, the man was ranting about the condition of their lawn.

They learned from another neighbor that the man, Jake, was a military veteran and very unfriendly to everyone. He lived alone; his wife had recently died, and his three children and their families lived far away. Leslie wondered if that were the reason behind Jake's crankiness and thought perhaps she would pay him a friendly visit later that week.

As the first few days in their new home passed, Tom spent most of his time at work or fixing things in the yard before dinner. Leslie was always home, having recently been laid off, so one day she decided to pay that friendly visit next door and say hello to Jake, hoping it would let him know they came in peace.

She knocked on the door and got a little scared when the door flew open and Jake stood there glaring at her. He grunted a "hello," and Leslie was about to speak when he began a tirade about how she and Tom had better cut down the tree branches that were hanging over his back fence. Then he dug into her about her car leaking oil and that she should never park it out on the street.

Leslie knew the difference between being understanding and being verbally abused. She held up her hand and yelled "Shut up!" so loud, Jake stopped mid-sentence. Leslie said she had come to offer friendship, but after seeing what kind of man he was, she didn't want anything to do with someone so mean and bitter.

She turned sharply on her heels and walked back to her house, slamming her front door closed. She tried to forget about the unpleasant incident and continue with her day.

Leslie didn't tell Tom about her battle with Jake, but it bothered her all night. She couldn't sleep, feeling like she had maybe said too much or gone too far. She thought, *Jake is nothing but a bitter, sick old man, and I should have just let it go.* She decided to pray for a while, hoping for a little guidance on how to bring a peaceful end to a bad situation before it escalated into a full-scale feud.

> *Do not judge, and you will not be judged; do not condemn, and you will not be condemned. Forgive, and you will be forgiven.*
>
> Luke 6:37

The next morning, the doorbell rang. Leslie answered it, surprised to see Jake standing there, holding something wrapped in foil. Her first instinct was that he had a bomb, but she invited him in anyway.

Jake sheepishly handed Leslie the foil package, and Leslie opened it to find a delicious-smelling cranberry loaf. Jake cleared his throat and asked Leslie to forgive him for being so hostile. Leslie invited him inside. They sat down at the kitchen table, and Leslie put on some coffee. Over the cranberry loaf, which Jake had baked himself from his wife's favorite recipe, he told her about his wife, Dina, and how much he missed her. He was sorry that his bitterness was affecting his behavior with his new neighbors. He wanted to start over. He hoped she would forgive him.

Leslie smiled, silently thanking God for this wonderful change of heart in Jake. She accepted his apology and then invited him to their first barbecue that weekend. Jake accepted with a big, happy smile and asked if he could help Tom with the grill. Seeing how something so small would make him so happy, Leslie said they would be glad to have their new neighbor and friend handle the grill. This would be the beginning of a tradition of summer barbecues. This would mark the start of a friendship.

God, I give thanks for the wisdom you share with me when I am trying to understand my own actions or someone else's. You know what is best, and you have my highest good in mind. I will turn to you for the advice and guidance I need. Thank you, God, for being a strong and loving presence in my life. Amen.

Forgiveness is the central virtue in God's treasure chest—God's forgiveness of us and our forgiveness of others and ourselves. At times we find that forgiveness comes very easily, even for grievous and painful hurts. But many times, we seem powerless to forgive, no matter how hard we try. This is when God's forgiving grace has the opportunity to touch and change us and then be extended to others through our examples.

Because none of us will ever be able to live a perfect life, we need to be understanding and practice forgiveness of others.

Lord, help us to move beyond the times we hurt one another, the times we willingly misunderstand, the times we cherish our differences, and the times we assume we know all there is to know about each other and turn away. Amen.

God knows that as hard as we may try, there are times when we will make human mistakes. Even so, if we trust in him and ask his forgiveness, he will bless us with mercy and peace.

The Lord hath spoken peace to my soul,
He hath blessed me abundantly,
Hath pardoned my sins;
He hath shown me great mercy and saved
    me by his love.
I will sing of his goodness and mercy while
    I live,
And ever, forever will praise his holy
    name.
O how sweet to trust in God,
And to know your sins forgiven,
To believe his precious word,
And be guided by his love.
Therefore goodness and mercy,
Shall follow me all the days of my life.
Amen.

C.E. Leslie, *Leslie's Crown of Song*

And Christ became a human being and lived here on earth among us and was full of loving forgiveness and truth.

John 1:14 TLB

Father, it's to you we come,
To pray for loved ones and for friends;
You offer mercy, grace, and peace,
And healing love that never ends.

Love is at the heart of all healing.

MOVING TOO FAST

The moment of impact went by in slow motion. Jamie felt as though she was trapped in a state of suspended animation as her small truck hit the red hatchback, sending her spinning around and around before slamming into the glass window of a storefront. It was raining and slick.

When the car stopped moving, she was frozen with shock. But she was alive and conscious. Jamie could hear the sirens and voices around her car, but she could not speak or move. It was as if life had been knocked out of her.

At the hospital, Jamie was tended to immediately. She lucked out with only a broken leg and a sprained wrist. After a few hours of sleep, she was finally able to talk with police and file a report, and that is when they told her about the other driver.

The young man had been seriously injured and was in surgery. Police had interviewed witnesses at the scene, and it was Jamie who had run a stop sign. In a daze, Jamie gave her version of the story, not denying it was her fault. She had been in a hurry to get to her job, having been late two days in a row. Her mind had been on her job and trying to find a good radio station on the dial.

Jamie knew in her heart that she had looked down momentarily and that in that moment she had possibly killed another human being. She felt terrible, racked with so much guilt.

Once her injuries were treated, Jamie was sent home with a friend. She called the hospital several times to check on the young man, whose name she learned was Brian. A nurse told her that Brian had several injuries, including internal bleeding. He would be in surgery for a while and then would need a lot of rest without interruption from visitors.

Throughout the night, Jamie tore herself apart with guilt, and the anguish made her so sick she vomited. She slept barely two hours the entire night, and first thing in the morning she asked her friend to drive her to the hospital, where she waited for hours to hear from someone about Brian's condition.

An older woman tapped her on the shoulder and introduced herself to Jamie as Brian's mother, Liz. She asked Jamie

The greatest gift we can offer someone is our forgiveness, for it has the dual power to set the other person free and to set us free as well.

how she was doing, and her concern and sincerity brought tears to Jamie's eyes. Jamie found herself apologizing over and over again, but Liz put her hand on Jamie's shoulder and told her Brian's surgery had gone well and he just needed to sleep a little while longer. She said that he was going to be okay.

An hour later, the nurse came by and told Liz that Brian could have visitors. As Liz was putting her book into her purse and picking up her coat to go see Brian, Jamie turned to Liz and asked if she could see Brian, and Liz smiled broadly and agreed.

Brian was in traction but awake. Liz introduced Jamie. Jamie cringed inside, waiting for his accusations, which she felt she truly deserved. But instead Brian smiled and said, "So you're the crazy woman who hit me. Thanks . . . I hated that car anyway." Jamie was stunned by the young man's kindness and lack of blame. She sat and talked with him for an hour, and she asked for his forgiveness, which he gave readily. When Jamie got ready to leave, Brian stopped her. He smiled at her and told her to do him a favor.

"Anything," Jamie said wholeheartedly.

"Forgive yourself. Accidents happen. Please don't beat yourself up about it," Brian said with a chuckle. "One of us in traction is enough, okay? Oh, and slow down, too. Life is too precious to speed through it."

Jamie promised and left the hospital in tears, but they were tears of joy for forgiving and having been forgiven.

God, grant me the courage to let go of shame, guilt, and anger. Free me of all negative energies, for only then will I become a conduit for joy and a channel for goodness. Amen.

The greater part of our happiness depends on our disposition and not our circumstances.

Martha Washington

Father, I need to understand that forgiveness is not dependent on my feelings but rather on a determination of my will. Help me to form a few well-chosen words of forgiveness. Amen.

Whenever you stand praying, forgive, if you have anything against anyone; so that your Father in heaven may also forgive you your trespasses.

Mark 11:25

Pray then in this way:
Our Father in heaven,
hallowed be your name.
Your kingdom come,
Your will be done,
on earth as it is in heaven.
Give us this day our daily bread.
And forgive us our debts,
as we also have forgiven our debtors.
And do not bring us to the time of trial,
but deliver us from the evil one.

Matthew 6:9–13

Dear Lord, we live in a broken world. We need your touch. Heal us of our prejudices, our sicknesses, our compulsions, our hatreds, and our shortsightedness. Help us to see people as you see them. For that matter, help us to see ourselves as you see us. Teach us to treat life as the gift you meant it to be. Keep us safe. Make us whole. Give us love to spare and forgiveness that can only come from you. Amen.

Are any among you suffering? They should pray. Are any cheerful? They should sing songs of praise. Are any among you sick? They should call for the elders of the church and have them pray over them, anointing them with oil in the name of the Lord. The prayer of faith will save the sick, and the Lord will raise them up; and anyone who has committed sins will be forgiven. Therefore confess your sins to one another, and

pray for one another, so that you may be healed. The prayer of the righteous is powerful and effective.

James 5:13–16

We find in the flight of butterfly wings
A message about more glorious things:
Take time to care, take time to smile,
For you, too, may linger for just a while.

He himself bore our sins in his body on the cross, so that, free from sins, we might live for righteousness; by his wounds you have been healed.

1 Peter 2:24

THE BRIDGE OF FORGIVENESS

Cecilia stood with a group of children at the Bridge of Forgiveness. The bridge is a learning tool at the museum where Cecilia works; they use it to teach about conflict resolution. Rising out of the floor, steep and somewhat uneven, the bridge can be difficult to cross, just as forgiveness can be difficult. But just as it is essential to cross the Bridge of Forgiveness to exit the gallery, it is also essential to forgive in order to grow and move on in life.

A little girl in a bright green shirt, her hair pulled into neat cornrows, raised her hand. "How can you forgive somebody if that person isn't sorry for what they've done?" she asked.

"It's not easy," Cecilia told her. "But think about it this way: If you keep hatred and resentment in your heart, you're only hurting yourself. Unless you let go of the pain, it will just keep haunting you."

The girl crossed her arms and frowned in disbelief. "What if they just go ahead and hurt you again? Like, what if they're mean and tease you?" Cecilia began to wonder if the girl had somebody in her class in mind and noticed that the girl gave a curt glance to a trendy, athletic boy who was smirking on the other side of the group.

"Maybe if you forgive that person, they'll stop hurting you," Cecilia said. The girl shook her head silently. The athletic boy nudged his neighbor and chuckled. "I wouldn't be telling you this if I didn't know it was true," Cecilia said. "It happened to me. Sit on the floor while I tell you a story."

Only when we are ready to relinquish the hurt is there an opportunity for forgiveness and healing to begin.

Cecilia told them all about Danny.

In high school, Cecilia was brainy and shy, a combination that attracted plenty of negative attention. Danny sat behind her in French class, and because of him Cecilia used to dread going to class. When she answered a question correctly, he'd kick her chair or poke her in the back with his sharpened pencil. When Cecilia turned around to hand him a paper, he'd make a snide remark.

Cecilia had learned a long time ago that it didn't help to tell the teacher about her problems. Any time she'd done that in a similar situation, it made the teasing worse.

Why is he picking on me? Cecilia would ask herself countless times. *I never did anything to him.* Cecilia had never said a mean word to him. It just wasn't fair.

Cecilia never could have predicted that a dream would change her life, but that's exactly what happened.

In the dream, Danny and Cecilia were sitting near the ocean together, relaxing in beach chairs, drinking fruit shakes, and enjoying the tropical breezes. The warm sun felt like an embrace, and Cecilia felt happy and calm. Without being told, Cecilia knew that Danny was one of her closest friends.

The next day, Cecilia saw Danny in the hallway. Usually when she saw him her stomach churned with fear, but this time she couldn't shake the peaceful feeling from her tropical dream. She smiled instead. Danny smiled back.

That day in French class, Cecilia answered questions and didn't receive any pokes or kicks from Danny. When she turned around to hand back a paper, she couldn't help seeing him as a friend. Danny didn't make a mean remark this time; he just grinned, and he never picked on her again.

When Cecilia had finished her story, the little girl's face grew thoughtful. The little girl glanced again at the athletic boy across the crowd.

"Now, I'd like everybody to cross the Bridge of Forgiveness," Cecilia announced. "And when you do, think about somebody you'd like to forgive or think about somebody you need to apologize to."

Before Cecilia had finished her sentence, the little girl in the green shirt led the way across the bridge, taking bold strides. At the end, she turned around, faced the athletic boy, and smiled.

Father, when we stand to cross the metaphorical bridge of forgiveness, please give us a little push to get us going. Amen.

If my people who are called by my name humble themselves, pray, seek my face, and turn from their wicked ways, then I will hear from heaven, and will forgive their sin and heal their land.

2 Chronicles 7:14

Lord God, the words "I'm sorry" and "forgive me" must be the most powerful in our vocabulary. May these phrases ever be poised on my lips, ready to do their work of release and restoration. I need to forgive, and I need to be forgiven. Let your healing balm wash over me, Father, as I both grant and receive the freedom that forgiveness brings. Amen.

Being sorry is the beginning of being forgiven. Being forgiven is the beginning of being free.

Lord, I need you to help me with the concept of forgiving people over and over again for the same behavior. I know you taught that there was no limit to the number of times we should forgive someone, but I get so weary of doing it, Lord. Help me to have a heart of forgiveness, so ready to forgive that I do so before the person who has wronged me even seeks my forgiveness. There's freedom in that kind of forgiveness, Lord. Help me to claim it for my own. Amen.

Let us be quick to forgive so that we may be quickly forgiven.

Living Gracefully

Let us therefore approach the throne of grace with boldness, so that we may receive mercy and find grace to help in time of need.

Hebrews 4:16

Do not sit down baffled by your difficulties and infirmities, but turn from them to claim Christ's abundant grace and strength, that at the end of life you may have done all that was set you to do, and more.

F.B. Meyer, *Our Daily Walk*

Amazing Grace!
How sweet the sound
That saved a wretch like me;
I once was lost, but now I'm found;
Was blind, but now I see.
'Twas grace that taught my heart to fear,
And grace my fears relieved;
How precious did that grace appear
The hour I first believed.
Through many dangers, toils and snares
I have already come,
'Tis grace that brought me safe thus far,
And grace will lead me home.

John Newton, "Amazing Grace"

For by grace you have been saved through faith.

Ephesians 2:8

Blest feast of love divine!
'Tis grace that makes us free
to feed upon this bread and wine,
in memory Lord of thee.
That blood which flowed for sin,
in symbols here we see,
and feel the blessed pledge within
that we are loved by thee.

Sir Edward Denny, *Blest Feast of Love Divine*

O God, mercy is not something we need to beg of you for your pleasure is to love us. Mercy, grace, and love are always available to us, Lord, for you are always available to us. We thank you. Amen.

ONE DAY AT A TIME

Ovarian cancer was not on Sandra's list of things to accomplish in her life. She had dreamt of a family, a career, and a happy and long life just like her parents had been blessed with. Being diagnosed with cancer at the age of 33 was not in the cards, at least not the deck she had chosen.

But now she was recovering from surgery and experiencing the horrible aftermaths of each chemotherapy treatment. Sandra sometimes didn't think she would survive another day, let alone another three months of the devastating treatments.

It had taken everything she had within her to get through the initial weeks of dealing with the diagnosis. The surgery had gone well but left her body racked with weakness, pain, and a serious need of rest. Still, she had kept her sanity so far, mainly by doing what a friend of hers in AA had told her.

She had begun to take life one day at a time.

It took a lot of strength of mind and courage, but each day Sandra struggled to stay focused on the moment at hand. At least a hundred times each day, she would find herself worrying about the future or regretting the past, and she would forcefully return her thoughts to the moment she was experiencing. And each time she did, she was surprised how much it helped her get through the pain and exhaustion of the chemo.

Hope is a mixture of perseverance and surrender.

Sandra knew that her future might not be set in stone, but instead of fearing the days ahead, she kept full attention on the day she was in. Her AA friend had given her one of his AA chips and told her, "If you can't take it one day at a time, then try ten minutes at a time," and on the really bad days when Sandra was sure she might not make it, she held that chip in her hand, clutching it like it was a holy object.

As her healing progressed, Sandra grew stronger and felt a little bit better, at least enough to start venturing out into the world more often. With each baby step, she made progress toward a level of wellness that, even though it might never be what it was before the cancer, was something she could deal with and even be grateful for.

With the help of loving friends, family, and her dedicated doctor, she was even able to begin a gentle exercise program. As her body became more powerful, she felt a newfound sense of empowerment occurring inside her as well.

Even when her doctor gave her a clean bill of health and said she was cancer-free, Sandra never went back to living as she had before. Now, more than ever, she knew the preciousness of each passing moment and continued to live her life one day at a time.

Spirit, help me to live one day at a time so that I may meet each day's challenges with grace, courage, and hope. Shelter me from the fears of the future and the anguish of the past. Keep my mind and heart focused on the present, where the true gift of happiness and healing is to be found. Amen.

Doctors know something about what a disease will do to a person. What they don't know is what a person may do to a disease.

In the midst of any illness lies a hidden opportunity to learn more about what we are made of.

On the way to Jerusalem Jesus was going through the region between Samaria and Galilee. As he entered a village, ten lepers approached him. Keeping their distance, they called out, saying, "Jesus, Master, have mercy on us!" When he saw them, he said to them, "Go and show yourselves to the priests." And as they went, they were made clean. Then one of them, when he saw that he was healed, turned back, praising God with a loud voice. He prostrated himself at Jesus' feet and thanked him. And he was a Samaritan. Then Jesus asked, "Were not ten made clean? But the other nine, where are they? Was none of them found to return and give praise to God except this foreigner?" Then he said to him, "Get up and go on your way; your faith has made you well."

Luke 17:11–19

Therefore I will boast all the more gladly about my weaknesses, so that Christ's power may rest on me. That is why, for Christ's sake, I delight in weaknesses, in insults, in hardships, in persecutions, in difficulties. For when I am weak, then I am strong.

2 Corinthians 12:9–10 NIV

Faith can help you to find purpose.

God, I pray to you today for the healing that only you can bring. I long to be free from pain and suffering, to be whole again in body, mind, and spirit. Give to me the soothing balm of your tender, loving care that I might mount up on wings of eagles and fly with ease again. Amen.

And after you have suffered for a little while, the God of all grace, who has called you to his eternal glory in Christ, will himself restore, support, strengthen, and establish you.

1 Peter 5:10

I asked God for strength that I might
   achieve;
I was made weak that I might learn to obey.

I asked for health that I might do great
   things;
I was given infirmity, that I might do
   better things.

I asked for riches that I might be happy;
I was given poverty that I might be wise.

I asked for power that I might have the
    praise of men;
I was given weakness that I might feel the
    need of God.

I asked for all things that I might enjoy
    life;
I was given life that I might enjoy all
    things.

I got nothing that I had asked for,
but everything that I had hoped for.

Almost despite myself my unspoken
    prayers were answered;
I am, among all men, most richly blessed.

prayer of an unknown Confederate soldier

When we pray for healing we pray for wholeness. Our prayers may be answered even if we don't receive exactly what we thought we asked for: The terminally ill person may be healed, yet not live; the chronically pained may still have physical suffering, yet their healing may mean they have been given an inner peace with which the physical problems are faced.

O Lord, please help me to understand that I won't always get what I pray for. In the same regard, I want to learn to thank you more for everything you do give me. Amen.

WHEN ALL ELSE FAILS, TRY HARDER

Gruff and barrel-chested, Coach had always demanded the best of his players and himself. During all his years of coaching football, a placard he had written by hand in block letters hung in the locker room, its letters fading and the corners curling from the steam of the showers. Its message was engraved in the minds of his players: "When All Else Fails, Try Harder."

In fact, Coach's tough demeanor and high standards did a good job of concealing how tenderhearted he was. That is, if you never saw him with his wife, Maizie. Former players who stopped in to see him after his retirement saw a new side of him as he cared for his wife.

One of Coach's most frequent visitors was a former player named John, who stopped in whenever he was home from college. The first time John visited, he was startled. He couldn't help noticing the contrast between Coach, still lively and fit, and his unhealthy wife. Lovely but white-haired and confined to a wheelchair, Maizie had suffered a series of strokes. Although she looked a good 10 years older than Coach, John eventually learned that the two were the same age and had been high school sweethearts.

Even when Maizie was having a bad day, her large dark eyes vague and her restless hands

Live in love, as Christ loved us and gave himself up for us, a fragrant offering and sacrifice to God.

Ephesians 5:2

fluttering, Coach referred to her as his "best girl" and included her in the conversation whether she responded or not. Often Coach and John played cards as they chatted. When Coach lost, he would inevitably take Maizie's hand and say, "Unlucky at cards, lucky at love." It was clear to John that Coach saw Maizie not as a helpless person humming tunelessly in a wheelchair but as the dark-eyed beauty who had caught his eye in a high school history class. Coach's one-syllable responses to John's hesitant questions made it clear that he was caring for his wife around the clock alone and wanted it that way.

One Christmas when John was home, it was obvious that Coach was having to take his own advice about trying harder. When John stopped by, the always confident Coach appeared sad and lost. Maizie was not there. Having suffered another stroke, she was back in the hospital. John and Coach chatted for a while, but Coach seemed preoccupied. He didn't ask the usual penetrating questions about John's football training and his grades. Coach looked tired and, for the first time, older. Once in a while he winced and rubbed his arm. Finally, glancing at his watch, he excused himself, saying that it was time for lunch at the hospital and he wanted to be sure Maizie ate well.

After John was back at school, his mother called. Coach had suffered a sudden fatal heart attack—but not until his wife was home from the hospital and a full-time nurse had been installed. When all else had failed, Coach had tried harder than he had ever asked any of his players to try. That powerful mind-body link he was always telling the team about had kicked in. He had hung on for Maizie until the time was better—not good, but better—for leaving her. John was grateful to have learned so early not only about football but also about life and heartbreak and the healing power of love.

Lord, we want to live life to its fullest. And although we know we shouldn't place our own wants before others' wants, it is so easy to think our dreams for the future matter most. Remind us to make compromises. Our love can get us further in this life than selfishness. Amen.

Do not be wise in your own eyes; fear the Lord, and turn away from evil. It will be a healing for your flesh and a refreshment for your body.

Proverbs 3:7–8

Heal me, O Lord.

Heal my heart, my soul, my body.

Heal anything in me that is wounded, less than whole.

Then guide me to live in a way that brings healing to others, too.

The Lord will guide you continually, and satisfy your needs in parched places, and make your bones strong; and you shall be like a watered garden, like a spring of water, whose waters never fail.

Isaiah 58:11

Heavenly Spirit, I long to be healed from my affliction, but I trust your will, your timing, and your plan for my life. I know that you will never give me more than I can handle and that you will always be there to help me. For this I am eternally grateful. Amen.

The grace of the living God refreshes like cool, clear water on a hot day, giving our parched souls the sustenance and nourishment they need.

TAKE ROOT

When joy and laughter vanish
Into illness and despair,
I remind myself that with God's help
You can get there from here.
So let not doubt and fear take seed
And grow into a tree,
But let God's healing make me whole
And love take root in me.

This is my commandment, that you love one another as I have loved you.

John 15:18

One there is, above all others,
well deserves the name of Friend;
his is love beyond a mother's,
costly, free, and knows no end;
they who once his kindness prove
find it everlasting love.

John Newton, *One There Is, Above All Others*

Finally, beloved, whatever is true, whatever is honorable, whatever is just, whatever is pure, whatever is pleasing, whatever is commendable, if there is any excellence and if there is anything worthy of praise, think about these things.

Philippians 4:8

THROUGH THE EYES OF A FRIEND

Different people nurture their friendships in different ways. Some friends are good listeners, and others always know when to send a card or gift. Some people exchange friendship bracelets or necklaces; others connect over the phone or through mail. On a recent shopping trip for a friend of hers, Olivia learned an incredible lesson about what lengths some people will go to nurture and support their friends. It's a lesson she won't soon forget.

One of Olivia's friends had new twin granddaughters who would soon be arriving from New Zealand. Olivia set off to find a gift for them and came upon a cute little boutique. As she browsed around, she couldn't help but notice the saleswoman, whom she later learned was a partner in the business. While wrapping a gift, the saleswoman was having a lively, yet intimate discussion with the only other shopper in the store.

"For as long as I've know you, Vella," the customer remarked, "I've never seen you with hair this short. It looks nice—but whatever prompted you to get a boy's haircut after all these years?"

Vella, who looked like she was in her early 50s, stopped wrapping and ran her hand through the crewcut stubble on her head. She started laughing, "If you think this is something, you should have seen me when I was bald!"

Everyone has something to give.

"Bald?"

Vella nodded with vigor. "Bald."

The customer looked skeptical. "What did you do, shave your head?"

"Yes, that's exactly what I did!" She returned to the chore at hand.

"What made you do that?"

Looking up from her work, Vella calmly and deliberately answered, "Cancer."

The customer gasped. "I had no idea you'd been sick. When did this happen?

Are you all right now?" she asked with genuine concern.

Vella smiled compassionately. "Not me—Jeanette; she's the one with cancer." She went on to explain that her dear young friend and business partner had been diagnosed with breast cancer and was being treated accordingly. "When she started chemotherapy and lost her hair, she was devastated. Claimed she was so ugly, no one would love her anymore." She shook her head. "Can you imagine such nonsense?"

"I think it would be traumatic for anyone," the customer said softly.

"Well, as it goes, I didn't know how to help her cope." Vella paused to bag the gift she had finished wrapping. After a deep breath, she continued, "One day, out of nowhere, I got the idea to lose my hair, too. It was the only way I could give Jeanette my support and show her that it didn't matter what she looked like on the outside. She was still the same wonderful person."

The customer's eyes widened. "That's unbelievable."

"I asked my husband and a few other close friends if they would shave their heads, too."

"And?"

"Seven of us showed up at the hospital that night with shiny, bald heads. The women taped pink bows on their scalps, and the men drew smiley faces on theirs. We all laughed and cried for a long time. But you know what? It worked. She's not afraid anymore."

"That's really wonderful. I'm sure Jeanette is thankful for what you did. You're an amazing friend." She made her way around the counter and hugged Vella, asked her to convey her best wishes to Jeanette, and bade her good-bye.

Vella proceeded to tidy up her work area as Olivia approached to pay for her gifts. After apologizing for listening in on the conversation, Olivia told Vella how deeply moved she was by her story. With tears welling up in her eyes, Olivia said, "You're a very special person. You take friendship to a higher level—one that most of us could never imagine."

"I just wanted to help my friend Jeanette through a difficult time," Vella said, smiling.

"Jeanette is very lucky to have a friend like you."

"No, I'm the lucky one," Vella said. "My friend is still alive."

Father, you help us to live gracefully by blessing us with wonderful friends. Thank you for making them as good as you are. Amen.

Bear one another's burdens, and in this way you will fulfill the law of Christ.

Galatians 6:2

*Let us approach with a true heart in full
assurance of faith, with our hearts sprinkled
clean from an evil conscience and our bodies
washed with pure water. Let us hold fast to
the confession of our hope without waver-
ing, for he who has promised is faithful.*

Hebrews 10:22–23

Your soul can dance though pain is here.

Call healing music to your ear.

Spot emotion's fickle turning,

Leap in love,

Stretch hopes,

Master fear's deep strains.

Dare to dance both health and pain.

However clumsy, long, or fleeting,

We dance life well if grace is leading.

Contributors

Marie D. Jones is an ordained minister and is widely published in books and magazines. She has contributed to *Mother's Daily Prayer Book, Bless This Marriage,* and *Simple Wisdom.*

Anne Broyles is a co-pastor who leads retreats on a variety of topics, such as family and women's spirituality. She is the author of many articles and books, including *Meeting God Through Worship* and *Journaling: A Spirit Journey.*

Rebecca Christian is a columnist and freelance writer who has written for *The Episcopalian* and National Catholic News Service. She has contributed to *Heartwarmers: Grandmas Always Have Time* and *Heartwarmers: Moms Are the Best.*

June Eaton is a writer and teacher who has published stories and articles in more than 50 Christian publications. She has also contributed to several books, including *Heartwarmers: Moms Are the Best* and *Charming Expressions: Angels.*

Susan Farr Fahncke is a freelance writer whose work regularly appears in *Whispers from Heaven* magazine. She contributed to *An Angel by Your Side* and the *Stories from the Heart* series.

Carol Smith is an inspirational writer with an M.A. in religious education. She has contributed to several religious books, including *Angels Watching Over Us* and *Angels: Heavenly Blessings.*

Natalie Walker Whitlock is a freelance writer whose work has appeared in *Family Fun* and *Woman's Day* magazines. She was coauthor of *Silver Linings: Friends* and a contributor to *Angels Watching Over Us.*

Acknowledgments

Publications International, Ltd., has made every effort to
locate the owners of all copyrighted material to obtain
permission to use the selections that appear in this book.
Any errors or omissions are unintentional; corrections, if
necessary, will be made in future editions.